Votewise

Helping Christians engage with the issues

Nick Spencer
Jubilee Centre, Cambridge

First published in Great Britain in 2004 by
Society for Promoting Christian Knowledge
36 Causton Street
London SW1P 4AU

The author and publisher have made every effort to ensure that the external
website and email addresses included in this book are correct and up to date at
the time of going to press. The author and publisher are not responsible for the
content, quality or continuing accessibility of the sites.

Scripture quotations taken from the HOLY BIBLE, NEW
INTERNATIONAL VERSION, copyright © 1973, 1978, 1984, International
Bible Society. Used by permission of Hodder & Stoughton Ltd, a member of
Hodder Headline Plc Group.

British Library Cataloguing-in-Publication Data
A catalogue record for this book is available from the British Library

ISBN 0–281–05683–8

1 3 5 7 9 10 8 6 4 2

Typeset by Avocet Typeset, Chilton, Aylesbury, Bucks
Printed in Great Britain by Bookmarque Ltd, Croydon, Surrey

Nick Spencer has worked as a researcher and writer for the Jubilee Centre and the London Institute for Contemporary Christianity since 2002, before which he was a consultant and researcher for The Henley Centre and Research International. His previous books include *Parochial Vision: The Future of the English Parish* and *Asylum and Immigration: A Christian Perspective on a Polarized Debate* (both published in 2004). He is married and has one daughter.

Contents

About the Jubilee Centre

The Jubilee Centre was founded by Michael Schluter in 1983 from a conviction that the biblical social vision is relevant to the contemporary world, providing a coherent alternative to modern political ideologies.

This vision initially led the Jubilee Centre into a number of campaigning roles, in partnership with others, on such issues as Sunday trading (Keep Sunday Special) and credit and debt (Credit Action). It also led to the launch of The Relationships Foundation in 1994 to engage in practical initiatives to reform society, based on a relational agenda or Relationism, on issues such as criminal justice, health, unemployment, business practice and peace building.

Over recent years the Jubilee Centre's focus has shifted away from campaigning towards promoting a coherent social vision based on careful research that applies biblical teaching to social, political and economic issues. It aims to share its work widely in order to equip Christians in the UK and overseas to shape society according to biblical principles.

The Jubilee Centre publishes its research regularly. Updates called *Engage* and Cambridge Papers are distributed free of charge each quarter. Bible study guides for each of the issues covered in this book are available on the Jubilee Centre website. For further information about the Jubilee Centre, to order or access other publications (most are available free of charge, including past Cambridge Papers) or to join our free mailing list, please visit <www.jubilee-centre.org> or contact us at:

Jubilee House
3 Hooper Street
Cambridge
CB1 2NZ

tel: 01223 566319
email: <info@jubilee-centre.org>

Foreword

How can we vote wisely? In particular, what is a Christian perspective on those issues that will face us at the next election?

'It's the economy, stupid.' So they say, but to vote primarily on the basis of a party's economic policy is indeed 'stupid'. Christ said, 'Life is more than food, and the body more than clothes.' So although we should look for food, jobs, higher levels of income and better public services from those we elect, that is not enough. To play a responsible role in the world, to heal the deep divisions among ourselves based on class, race or religion, to feel at peace within ourselves, we need a bigger vision, a greater dream.

Martin Luther King had a dream in 1967 for the future of the USA. It was a dream of racial harmony where black and white would live and work together in communities, schools and government without fear or favour. It was a profoundly Christian dream, for it was a dream of right relationships – relationships of harmony, truth, justice and love.

Christianity is a 'relational religion'. Whether one looks at the language of covenant and atonement, at the meaning of the cross as reconciliation between God and humankind, at love as the basis of Christian ethics, or at 'knowing God' as the essence of eternal life, relationships is the category in which Christian thinking is expressed. The research of the Jubilee Centre over the last 20 years has sought to demonstrate how this central theme of relationships can be applied to the key issues of public life, such as education, health, economics, finance, criminal justice and immigration.

In this incisive, short book, Nick Spencer builds on this research to present a fresh perspective on the issues facing Britain as we approach the next election – a perspective built on a relational understanding of both public and private life. If you believe the world would be a better place if we focused our attention on relational rather than on financial perspectives, this book will help you see the coming election with fresh eyes, and discover once more that it is possible for Christians to hope for a better tomorrow.

Michael Schluter
Chairman, Jubilee Centre
Cambridge

Acknowledgements

This book is essentially a team effort, drawing on 20 years of social and biblical research and analysis by the Jubilee Centre.

Footnotes regularly record debts owed but I would like to highlight several at this juncture. Much of the overall thinking and particularly those sections outlining biblical perspectives draw on *Jubilee Manifesto* (IVP, forthcoming), to whose many contributors I am grateful. In particular, I should mention Jonathan Burnside's work on immigration and criminal justice, and Paul Mills's on the economy.

Michael Schluter, whose overall input to the task of developing a biblical social vision has been enormous, was a rich source of ideas and guidance, and Jason Fletcher provided his usual wise counsel regarding sense and structure. Ann Holt commented incisively and helpfully on the education chapter. John Ashcroft has been an inexhaustible supply of intelligent and helpful comments and has influenced the content more than anyone else. Alison Barr from SPCK helped steer the book from inception to publication with much thought and consideration.

I am grateful to all these people for their contributions, which have vastly improved the manuscript. Any remaining errors are mine alone.

I am also grateful to all the Jubilee Centre's supporters without whom neither this book nor the research behind it would have been possible.

The book is dedicated to my brother David, who has shown me more about personal courage and resilience than anyone else I know.

Nick Spencer
London

Introduction:
Politics, Politicians and the Public Today

Won't vote. Might march

Fifty-nine per cent of the UK electorate went to the polls on 7 June 2001. It was the lowest turnout since 1918 and 12 per cent less than the already low figure of 1997. The Prime Minister received fewer votes than Neil Kinnock did when he lost the 1992 general election. Overall, 11 million people voted for Tony Blair and 33 million did not.[1] As election victories go, it was the most Pyrrhic of modern times.

The year 2001 was not an anomaly. Local election turnouts hover around one in three. Thirty-eight per cent of the eligible population voted in the Welsh Assembly elections and 49 per cent in the Scottish Parliament ones. The UK consistently has one of the lowest turnout rates for elections to the European Parliament, with returns of 24 per cent in 1999 and, with the aid of postal voting in some areas, 39 per cent in 2004.

Such disengagement has caused much soul-searching. William Hague said in the wake of his 2001 defeat:

> All of us in the House, in all parties, should be chastened by levels of voter apathy [. . .] Elections to this place should be the cornerstone of democratic accountability in our country, yet millions of people are not sufficiently motivated to take part in them. The blunt truth is that people increasingly see politics and Parliament as remote from their lives. They do not think that they matter.[2]

For a more detailed analysis of the issues discussed in this chapter see Nick Spencer, *Apolitical Animals? A Biblical Perspective on Engaging with Politics in Britain Today* (Cambridge: Jubilee Centre, 2003: <www.jubilee-centre.org>).

Yet, the last five years have also seen the two largest demonstrations in British political history, in the anti-war and Countryside Alliance marches of February 2003 and September 2002 respectively. They have seen fuel protests bring the nation to a standstill, anti-capitalist marches turn into riots, demonstrations against student top-up fees, and the destruction of genetically modified (GM) crops. While fewer people are voting, more are marching.

The reasons behind these trends are complex and have kept commentators in column inches for years. According to one post-general election survey, 21 per cent of people said they 'couldn't get to the polling station because it was too inconvenient', and 16 per cent said they didn't vote because they 'were away on election day' – explanations that have a ring of 'the dog ate my homework' about them.[3] Equally specifically, Labour's 179-seat majority acted as a powerful disincentive to voters in 2001: those who had voted Labour in 1997 thought there was no need to vote, and those who hadn't thought there was no point.

The reasons for public disengagement are much deeper than the circumstances of June 2001, however, and divide into three categories: politics, politicians and the public.

In their study of the 2001 election for the 19th British Social Attitudes (BSA) report, Catherine Bromley and John Curtice came out heavily for the first category.[4] 'Turnout fell in 2001,' they concluded, 'because the choice that the electorate was being asked to make was not sufficiently interesting, rather than because a wave of apathy and alienation has descended upon the electorate.' There is much truth in this. The lie of the political landscape, as we shall see in Chapter 1, shifted significantly in the 1990s, and the general tenor of Labour's first term in power, exemplified by their courting of big business and reduction in the basic rate of income tax, further blurred traditional political boundaries. For many voters it became hard to distinguish one party's policies from another's. As one respondent told a post-election study, 'I didn't vote this time because the parties all seemed the same.'[5]

If politics has bred confusion, politicians have provoked hostility. The 1990s saw governments mired by accusations of deceit and corruption. As sleaze dogged John Major's administration, spin has marked Tony Blair's. The situation has not been helped by the soap-opera mentality that has developed around Westminster. Human-interest stories attract larger audiences than policy documents, and in their desire to appeal to a population that lives on a diet of TV entertainment and believes itself to be too busy to absorb anything longer than a soundbite, politicians and the media have sometimes conspired to transform Westminster into a gilt version of Walford. Not surprisingly the electorate has grown increasingly cynical and mistrusting of politicians (not to mention journalists).

Yet the electorate itself is hardly blameless. As even Bromley and Curtice acknowledge, British political disengagement implicates Britons as well as their political system. BBC research into voter apathy conducted in February 2002 reported that 37 per cent of respondents said they felt 'powerless', 'unsupported' and 'unrepresented'.[6] At the same time, other studies have shown that the number of people who actively *do something about this* remains consistently low.[7] The percentage of people who claim they have engaged in some form of non-electoral political activity over the last 12 months has increased in every category since the 1980s but, with the exception of signing a petition, no category engages more than one in six people.[8] Our consumer culture may incite us to complain when our political 'service' is unsatisfactory, but it does not encourage us to do much more.

These three reasons – confusion with politics, disaffection with politicians and aversion to engagement – have prepared the way for single-interest politics. 'Causes' are more straightforward than mainstream politics. They are more obviously relevant to my interests. Involvement in them bypasses the official and labyrinthine paths of action. It also circumvents the 'powerlessness' implicit in being one of 50,000 (or 500,000) constituency voters. If I detest MPs, don't understand Parliament and can't be bothered to learn about Westminster, I can at least join a march or write to the press.

We may be some way from being a nation of single-issue political activists, but our disengagement with Westminster and our reported willingness to take such steps suggest that things may be changing.

Joined-up politics

The question we need to ask is whether this actually matters. If those who are drifting from mainstream politics are gradually adopting single issues, should we not just go with the flow?

To some extent the answer is 'Yes'. Single-issue campaigns, where they exist, can be organic, relevant and committed. They are politics in its purest sense of balancing the conflicting interests of people and causes within a gathered community, rather than a distant and professionalized activity conducted by a minority on behalf of the majority.

Yet there are good reasons to have a vision for and engage in 'mainstream' politics too. For one, we can only start from where we are. Single-issue politics may, in time, reshape the mainstream, but the next election, and with it the way we address current social problems, will be decided according to the existing political system. To ignore present political debates entirely in favour of local concerns is to renounce the responsibility that many people claim to feel as participants within a democracy.

More profoundly, single-issue causes can disunite just as much as they unite. When the then Czech president, Vaclav Havel, invited anti-globalization protestors to debate with International Monetary Fund (IMF) officials during the Prague summit in 2000, he recognized that thousands of single-issue campaigns could (and did) produce thousands of (mutually contradictory) solutions, none of which was remotely as powerful as the forces it confronted. By their very nature such causes are limited and specific, commonly unable to stretch across issue boundaries and achieve the joined-up thinking that is so important to many issues. Campaigning on asylum, for example, is right and just but ineffective if unable to engage with the related issues of international order, transport and community, education and cultural awareness. For such complex, interconnected issues, a uniting vision promises perspective, motivation and the prospect of effectiveness.

In addition, the generally low levels of non-electoral political participation disguise significant imbalances within the population.[9] Education correlates very strongly with participation: the higher one's qualifications, the more likely one is to have undertaken some form of non-electoral activity, such as contacting an MP or the media or joining a campaign group. Self-confidence, political understanding and scepticism all encourage activism. The result is that the politically ignorant, ill-educated and insecure, among whom are the most vulnerable members of society, become progressively voiceless.

Finally, from a Christian's point of view, democracy implies individual accountability before God in a way that other political systems do not. With the rights of electoral participation come the responsibilities for national action, and although individual voters will not be as answerable for national policies as their executive, the democratic process does confer a duty on them as much as it does a right. The fact that we describe politicians as *our* leaders is surely significant.

None of these reasons should deter single-issue campaigns or other forms of non-electoral activity, but they do remind us that we abandon mainstream politics at a cost. A heartfelt concern for others will prompt us to channel the commitment we might otherwise expend on immediate, localized concerns towards the good of society as a whole.

Votewise: engaging with the issues

This book is an attempt to guide that commitment in advance of the next general election. It makes no pretence of being a comprehensive analysis of current political issues, nor is it a covert strategy to grab the Christian vote for a particular party.

Instead, it tries to steer people away from personality and party politics towards the issues that underlie them both. Spin, sound-bites and ratings are the death of serious political engagement. The fact that a nation's future can be decided by the appearance, hair-cut or smile of a party leader is worrying. The fact that it can be shaped by the public's opinion of a party's image, reputation or supporters is hardly less disturbing.

This is not to say that the role of politicians is inconsequential. The perceived honesty, integrity and reliability of a potential Prime Minister and his or her colleagues are crucially important. As we have been reminded on countless occasions in recent years, a party's policies matter not a jot if its politicians are untrust-worthy. There is, however, a fundamental difference between voting for a politician because she has a good image and voting for her because she is unlikely to renege on her manifesto pledges.

Those pledges are unavailable at the time of writing, but even if they were, there is good reason not to engage with them directly. Manifestos are policies dressed up as promises.[10] It can be fiendishly difficult to understand exactly what they propose, which is why John Humphrys and his colleagues have such vital roles to play at election time. No book can hope to provide the detailed, insistent, inquisitorial scrutiny of the *Today* programme.

A book can, however, wrest the initiative from party manifestos by helping the voter to think through the issues and ask the questions that matter to her. Accordingly, *Votewise* adopts for its structure the 'most important issues facing Britain today', as recorded by the polit-ical monitor of the Market and Opinion Research Institute (MORI). This monthly survey asks respondents what they think is 'the most important issue [. . . and] other important issues facing Britain today' and uses the results to track the public's dominant con-cerns. Such polls are not perfect, as respondents' answers can reflect the headline of the moment or what they think they *should* be con-cerned about. Yet, the frequency of the survey and the fact that people answer in their own words, rather than being given categories to tick, make it one of the best guides to the nation's concerns.

Over the course of the last parliamentary term (up until the summer of 2004), the most important issues have been health and the National Health Service (NHS); education and schools; defence, foreign affairs and terrorism; crime, law and order; race, asylum and immigration; Europe and the European Union (EU); the economy; pensions; and transport.[11] The fact that two of the most pressing issues currently facing the world, environmental degradation and international poverty, do not make it on to the list is testimony to the natural and problematic parochialism of national politics. While both issues are briefly touched upon in this book, their general omission reflects the realistic agenda of the next general election, rather than any definitive statement about the most important social and political issues of the age.

These issues comprise the central chapters this book, with several categories elided for reasons of space and overlap, and the final order reflecting partly the increasing importance attached by the public to each issue, and partly a general movement from specific to more inclusive issues.[12]

Each chapter has three functions that divide it into roughly equal sections. The first outlines the contours of the debate. Just because people deem an issue one of the most important of the day, it does not mean they understand it. Indeed, sometimes it is quite the opposite: asylum and immigration are considered important at least in part because we do *not* understand the issues and consistently overestimate the number of asylum seekers and immigrants resident in the UK. The first section of each chapter uses up-to-date social and political research to inform and clarify the debate, and to draw attention to its key questions.

The chapter then turns to biblical teaching for a Christian perspective on the issue in hand. The history of political theology is long, complex and peppered with notoriously difficult questions: What is the right role of the state? How far should the Church be 'political'? What is the relative weight of the Old and New Testaments? Because these fascinating but difficult questions would detain us for too long, they are studiously avoided in favour of a more issue-focused approach that draws on the entire biblical canon and, to a more limited degree, later theological thinking. A sensitive reading of biblical material offers a wealth of ideas and principles that are directly and indirectly relevant to current debates, and the middle part of each chapter offers a necessarily brief analysis of this material.

A sensitive reading is not enough, however, and the final section of each chapter attempts to synthesize the biblical material with its relevant contemporary issue. These sections do not detail *the* Christian position on these issues, an all but impossible challenge even without the space limitations, nor do they tell the reader which party is closest to this mythical position. Whereas Christians should (hopefully) agree on the principles that underpin and shape policies, the policies themselves can be so specific, indeterminate and technical that those who share principles will naturally differ over which policies most effectively implement them.

Each chapter's final section therefore offers a series of principles against which readers might evaluate party manifestos and promises. Some of these principles nod tentatively in the direction of specific policies and others away from them. Yet, no final section attempts the hubristic task of outlining the definitive Christian stance on an issue.

Accordingly, no chapter makes any pretence of being the last word on the topic and each finishes with a list of books, papers and websites by means of which readers might engage further in the issues discussed. While the specific objective is to help readers understand and critique electoral issues, the book recognizes that political participation begins rather than ends at the ballot box.

Overall, the central chapters hope to break the surface of the election debate and identify the real choices that underlie the rhetoric. They aim to equip Christians to engage more confidently in the election and in subsequent political debates, encouraging them to break down the sacred–secular divide which sees God relegated to Sunday worship and barred from the choices which shape society and our everyday lives.

This analysis of the issues and the electoral process as a whole should also be treated as an occasion for self-examination. Elections are not simply a matter of voters sitting in judgement on their elected politicians, but an opportunity for them to ask themselves: How should we live now? Decisions made at election time affect the kind of society we live in, but they also constitute a personal ideological statement. We may not buy into big political visions much these days, but the manner in which we vote and engage in the electoral process cannot help but be a statement of personal belief.

Historically, the available statements have been limited and distinct, with Christians being found on each side of the debate. Today, they are no less limited but rather less clear-cut, and it is with an examination of the shifting positions that form the political backdrop today that we start.

❶ Political Ideas Today

It used to be so easy. You were either for individualism, small government and the free market or for collectivism, big government and nationalization. The answer to the UK's problems was to reduce government interference and allow families and businesses to run their own affairs, or to redistribute wealth from the affluent to the needy and let the state run industry. You were motivated by choice and freedom or by fairness and equality. There was ground in between these positions but it was a political no-man's land, sparsely populated and exposed to both sides.

Barely 20 years ago, voters could choose between a manifesto which promised to 'return public industries [. . .] to public ownership [. . .] prepare a five-year national plan [. . .] to rebuild British industry [. . . and] open immediate negotiations [. . .] for Britain's withdrawal from the EEC', and one which promised to 'expose state-owned firms to real competition [. . .] transfer more state-owned businesses to independent ownership [. . . and] lower taxes on capital and savings'. Even the anodyne and rhetorical language of party manifestos (every manifesto calls for 'a fairer, better future for all') could not disguise the significant policy differences.

The last 20 years have seen the British political landscape change beyond all recognition. The middle ground, having once been a scarred and empty no-man's land, is now positively congested with policies and politicians, the majority of whom are migrants from the economic left. In a study of Margaret Thatcher's and Tony Blair's success in shaping the political landscape, the National Centre for Social Research demonstrated that, in spite of popular belief, and somewhat ironically, 'Mr Blair appears to have been more successful in achieving Mrs Thatcher's objective of moving the country towards her views', than she was.[1]

The result is a 'middle ground' that is clearly right of centre, a kind of 'Thatcher Lite' as it has been dubbed. The free market has triumphed over the state, and government's job is now to facilitate business rather than dictate to it. The idea of preparing 'a five-year national plan [. . .] to rebuild British industry' is anathema.

The left–right axis is a useful tool but inadequate in itself, being limited to economic issues. To understand the political landscape requires a second dimension: the libertarian–authoritarian axis. This measure deals with attitudes to authority, with one end favouring conformity, obedience and traditional morality, and the other stressing the importance of individualism and moral freedom and being reluctant to impose conditions on the way people live their lives.

Since 1986 British public opinion has shifted away from authoritarianism to the middle ground and, to a slightly lesser extent, from the middle ground towards libertarianism.[2] The result is a society increasingly dominated by a 'soft libertarianism' that is, for example, more positive towards homosexual practice and the legalization of cannabis but strongly opposed to harder drugs and criminal activity.

This has been reflected in party-political stances. The Conservatives' 'war on single mothers' (to use Theresa May's unfortunate phrase) and their 'Back to Basics' campaign mark the grave of their 'intervention' in people's lives. Labour's recent interest in obesity and smacking show that such 'intervention', either on moral or on health grounds, is not entirely dead. In general, since the mid-1990s, both major parties have been falling over themselves to appear tolerant and inclusive in areas of personal behaviour while wanting to sound tough on crime and anti-social behaviour, in such a way as to appeal to an increasingly soft-libertarian public.

These two moves – towards 'Thatcherism Lite' and soft libertarianism – have seen new battle lines drawn, and although these are sometimes difficult to identify in politics' crowded middle ground, they tend to cluster around the popular, if vexed, issue of responsibility for public services. If government's role is to enable business to create wealth, and individuals to enjoy their lives, who has responsibility for ensuring the public services – health, education, security, transport – that are necessary for both?

The historic answers to this question – the state (by tax and welfare provision) or individuals (by moral, family-based, 'respectable' lives) and companies (by the discipline of the free market) – are less convincing in the new political landscape. The new answers are where the current battle lines have been drawn.

One such line runs through the question of 'choice' and 'localism'. This appears, at first, to be an area of consensus. All three main parties recognize that responsibility for and delivery of public services need to move away from central government towards the consumers and service providers on the ground, whether that be local authorities, communities, voluntary organizations or individuals. In the words of one recent commentator:

> Each [of the main parties . . .] is straining to establish its credentials as the natural home of the 'new localism'. For New Labour, several ministers have now acknowledged the limits of command-and-control approaches to reform. For the Conservatives, Michael Howard used his inaugural speech as leader to reassure voters that he would 'cut the fly-by-wire controls that lead straight back to a dashboard in Whitehall Central [and] stifle initiative and innovation'. And for the Liberal Democrats, Charles Kennedy has proposed scrapping five entire departments. His rationale: 'Save at the centre to get more help and services for people in the local community.[3]

Yet beneath the consensus, there are differences. First, there is the question of the balance between local responsibility and national equity: are we prepared to let some local services fail in the quest to decentralize responsibility or will we ensure a minimum national level that will necessitate interference and some control remaining in Westminster? To a degree, this is the old battle of freedom vs. equality, played out in a particular corner of public service provision.

Second, and linked to this issue of localizing responsibility for public services, is the role of the public itself. The traditional libertarian view that I can smoke, drink, eat, drive, and generally live however I like without government interference is ultimately untenable in a society that wishes to maintain an extended welfare system like the UK's.

This is becoming clearest in the area of health, where people's 'right' to binge drink, overwork, sleep around and eat unhealthily is putting unsustainable pressure on the NHS.[4] But it is also an issue for transport policy (can we afford an unlimited right to drive?), education (can teachers be expected to educate children without parental support?), and public safety (can we ignore identity cards and citizenship pledges with the present threat of terrorism?). In the same way as the current battle over public-service responsibility replays the old debate between freedom and equality, the role of the public in these services is a microcosm of the traditional authoritarian vs. libertarian debate: can government insist on an individual's 'co-operation' and threaten to limit their access to public services as an inducement, or should it respect the individual's choices at whatever cost?

Beneath these two debates is a third that receives less airtime during elections but underlies all political positions. The homogenization of the political landscape and the (supposed) death of ideological politics mean that the question, *What is your vision for society?* is rarely answered except in the most superficial and rhetorical way. All party leaders always want a just, fair, free and prosperous future for all.

Such have-it-all rhetoric tends to dissolve when faced with specific questions. Political visions may wish to be attractively inclusive, but to be meaningful they must be specific, and this demands a degree of prioritization. What is our primary goal as a society? Do we want social equality? If so, at what cost? Alternatively, do we want economic growth, and again, if so, at what cost?

The last 20 years have seen the demise of the social-equality agenda as a wholly independent and autonomous programme. No Western government is prepared to engineer the economic equality of its citizens at any cost. The quest for social equality today

survives under the roof of economic growth: if the latter is cur-
tailed, the former will lose momentum. Only by creating wealth
will we be able to generate equality.

Yet there are signs that this 'growth vision' is itself falling apart.
More and more research is showing that money does not bring
happiness, let alone equality.[5] The singular pursuit of affluence
becomes counterproductive after a certain point, damaging those
things, such as family, security, stability and environment, which
make life worthwhile. The growth vision is in danger of becoming a 'growth fetish'.

If the cracks that are appearing in our dominant economic
vision have the same effect as those that damaged the social-equality visions in the 1980s and 1990s, the very foundations of the
political landscape will be shaken. Debates about freedom, equality, authority and liberty will carry on but will be liable to wholesale redefinition as political foundations shift and the British ask
themselves afresh: What, exactly, do we want as a society?

The question that Christians face at the next election and
beyond is, therefore, not just: What is the correct position to assume
along the existing political battle lines? but: Does Christianity offer
a vision that could stabilize the very foundations of the political
enterprise?

Before we address these questions, we must briefly touch on
another area that will, rightly, be central to the next election.

Events, dear boy

A young journalist once asked Harold Macmillan what he thought
was the greatest difficulty about being Prime Minister. After paus-
ing for effect, the PM famously replied, 'Events, dear boy. Events.'
Tony Blair would probably agree.

The focus groups that were so influential during Labour's first
term in office told the government that transport was relatively
unimportant to the public. Towards the end of that term, a surprisingly well-organized fuel protest brought the country to a

standstill. Thereafter, rail accidents at Hatfield, Potters Bar and Selby, combined with an earlier disaster at Ladbroke Grove, the introduction of congestion charges in London and several other cities, and on-going discussions about airport expansion, conspired to make transport one of the keys issue of Labour's second term. The government was ill prepared and suffered accordingly.

In the year before Labour came to power, there were 29,600 applications for asylum in the UK. By 1999, this figure had risen to 71,000 and three years later it stood at 84,000.[6] The reaction to this increase verged on the hysterical in some quarters. Asylum applicants were demonized as bogus and scroungers, and the Blair government, criticized for being a 'soft touch', responded with tough policy initiatives and tougher rhetoric. The issue has remained central to voters' concerns.

The al-Qaeda attacks on America in September 2001 utterly changed global politics. Subsequent invasions of Afghanistan and Iraq, precipitated and 'justified' by the 9/11 atrocities, dominated Labour's second term. A dubious report on Radio 4's *Today* programme and the suicide of Dr David Kelly led to the highly publicized and controversial Hutton Inquiry that, despite exonerating the government, failed to quell criticism. Event followed event and, although some were clearly self-inflicted, they still managed to wrong-foot Labour and distract it from its public-sector reform programme.

Failure to cope with such 'events' has weakened many a government, turning its grand vision for Britain's future into a frantic exercise in fire-fighting and damage limitation. Post-ideological, pragmatic politics may be popular, but is inherently vulnerable to such circumstances: it is difficult to establish 'what works' in a crisis.

An ideologically rooted political vision may not be much more successful in coping with a national disaster, but it does, at least, have clearly articulated principles on which it can draw in such situations.

A Christian vision*

Is there, then, a compelling Christian vision for politics?

Libraries have been filled with attempted answers to this question and a small sample of such books is given in the 'Further engaging' section below. The (all too brief) answer offered here draws heavily on the work of the Jubilee Centre and begins with the uncontroversial observation that Christianity is a relational religion.

The vision at the start of the biblical narrative is of man, woman and the rest of creation relating to one another and to their creator in a harmonious and fulfilling way. The subsequent 'fall' ruptures these relationships, marking them with disobedience, fear, blame, toil and pain. The resolution of the rupture comes in the incarnation, when God and man are fused in Jesus of Nazareth, whose life and work was to heal relationships and re-incorporate wholeness or *shalom* into creation. The narrative ends with a vision of a city in which creation and creator live and rejoice together in right relationship. From beginning to end, relationships dominate the Christian story.

Right relationships are made possible through the self-emptying love that Christ demonstrated in his life and teachings. Love is the object of life, the goal of creation and the foundation of the moral order. Human beings are here to 'love the Lord [. . .] with all your heart [. . .] soul [. . .] mind and [. . .] strength [and] love your neighbour as yourself'.[7] The incarnation, crucifixion and resurrection reveal and restore the created order of love, 'making all things new'.[8]

While attractive, this may seem irrelevant to any potential political vision. Our modern concepts of love and relationships have been so thoroughly personalized, romanticized and sexualized that the idea that they might have something to contribute to public policy seems strange. Yet, biblical teaching has a broader and more

---

* This section draws heavily on Michael Schluter *et al.*, *Jubilee Manifesto: A Framework, Agenda and Strategy for Social Reform* (Leicester: IVP, 2005).

hard-headed understanding of relationships and of the conditions that build or destroy them.

Relationships exist not just between man and woman or parent and child, but also between supplier and customer, doctor and patient, native and immigrant, teacher and pupil, victim and criminal, governor and governed, and welfare provider and recipient, and a model for many of these relationships lies in the history and experience of the people of God.[9] This ranges through personal, familial, constitutional, judicial, economic, territorial and international concerns, exploring and directing what shapes a healthy society, always with the underlying assumption that 'God measures a society [. . .] not by the size of its GNP or by the efficiency of its markets, but by the quality of its relationships'.[10]

Thus biblical teaching speaks of the willing, open, mutual commitment inherent in the idea of covenant that underpins statehood or nationhood. It articulates a principle of subsidiarity, in which central government is responsible for only those roles that cannot be discharged effectively at a more local level, in such as way as to encourage localized responsibility and direct political involvement.

Its vision is of a national unity that is built on a system of law and education, and informed by shared values and aspirations, rather than on military or executive centralization. It sees the (extended) family as the basis of social cohesion, recognizing in it an economic and welfare, as well as an emotional and educational, role.

It sees property and a sense of rootedness as the foundation of stable communities and social capital. It views crime not so much as the individual breaking the state's rules but more as a relational breakdown between offender and victim, or between offender and community.

It embraces money as a means of enjoying creation, but insists it be used a tool of a relationally focused society rather than being a goal in itself. Overall, it sees individual behaviour and national, social structures as underpinned by values of loyalty, faithfulness, justice, *shalom* or wholeness, mercy and wisdom, rather than modern ones of choice, freedom, prosperity and equality (which is not to say, of course, that these values are unimportant).

These principles offer a relational model for politics but, importantly, are embodied in a living community that underwent significant changes over a period of centuries. The on-going moral and political failures that marked Israel's history, the powerful and persistent prophetic critique, the trauma and re-evaluation of exile, and, most importantly, the incarnation of the Christ and commissioning of his Church each provide lenses through which we read and apply the principles outlined above.

A direct translation of biblical narrative to twenty-first-century Britain is unacceptable. Not only do we need to observe a careful process of decontextualizing principles but we must also engage sensitively in developing a framework for implementing them. What, for example, are the appropriate covenant principles for the UK today? What is the right balance between central and local responsibility? What does the idea of rootedness demand from individuals, employers and the state? How should principles of relational justice and restoration be applied to criminal justice today?

These are hard questions, but that is no objection in itself. Relational principles tread carefully between the well-entrenched lines of authoritarianism and libertarianism, and between economic freedom and equality. Relationships benefit from, but are not predicated on, wealth or economic parity. They eschew the individualism inherent in libertarianism, but also reject the more dehumanizing aspects of authoritarianism. Instead, relational thinking makes a tool of wealth creation and economic equity, just as it does of individual responsibility and respect for authority. All are used for the goal of optimizing relationships across society.

This, then, is the overarching principle of the central chapters of this book. As outlined in the Introduction, these chapters examine the issues that are likely to dominate the next election campaign. None is definitive or prescriptive, and the more policy-specific they are, the greater scope there is for debate and disagreement.

They will not make up readers' minds for them, but they will, it is hoped, equip them to understand, critique and engage with the big issues facing the UK today from a Christian point of view that is, ultimately, about relationships.

Further engaging

Publications

Craig Bartholomew *et al.*, *A Royal Priesthood: The Use of the Bible Ethically and Politically* (Carlisle: Paternoster, 2002)

Oliver O'Donovan, *The Desire of Nations: Rediscovering the Roots of Political Theology* (Cambridge: Cambridge University Press, 1999)

Michael Schluter *et al.*, *Jubilee Manifesto: A Framework, Agenda and Strategy for Christian Social Reform* (Leicester: IVP, 2005)

Christopher Wright, *Old Testament Ethics for the People of God* (Leicester: IVP, 2004)

Websites

Christians in Politics: <www.christiansinpolitics.org.uk>

Christian Peoples Alliance: <www.cpalliance.net>

Christian Socialist Movement: <www.christiansocialist.org.uk>

Conservative Christian Fellowship: <www.ccfwebsite.com>

Green Party: <www.greenparty.org.uk>

Liberal Democrat Christian Forum: <www.christianforum.libdems.org>

❷ Asylum

'Stop this Asylum Madness Now', roared the *Sun*'s front page in August 2003. 'There is a timebomb ticking in our midst', the paper told its readers. '[It] must be defused.'[1] 'Stop pretending asylum-seekers are a problem', cried the *Independent* around the same time. 'Playing this crude numbers games plays into the hands of xeno-phobes.'[2]

Few topics divide opinion quite as much as asylum. There is, it seems, no middle ground. Asylum seekers are either a threat to our liberty or an unqualified blessing. Caricatures of new-trainer-wearing, mobile-phone-carrying benefit-scroungers, or dignified freedom fighters who deserve to be rewarded for having the initiative to make it to the UK, abound. Political opponents are dismissed as either whinging liberals or crypto-racists, and constructive debate is slowly suffocated under the weight of polemic.

Such rancorous squabbling is unhealthy. Many people are understandably anxious at the idea of public services being exploited by 'benefit tourists' or of English becoming a second language in schools and local authorities, but this apprehension can cloud rather than clarify the debate.

Public perception is often woefully inaccurate, fuelling the anx-iety that the polarized and antagonistic public 'debate' does little to address. Asylum seekers (i.e. people who have fled their country of origin and submitted a claim for asylum in another country) are regularly confused with refugees (people who reside outside their country of origin owing to a well-founded fear of being persecuted),[3] who are confused with 'illegal immigrants' (people who reside outside their country of origin but without the legal warrant of their country of residence), who are confused with 'immigrants' (a notoriously slippery term without any definitive definition but usually read as people who settle as permanent or long-term residents in a different country). All too often, it is easier to have passionate opinions than to understand and use terms correctly.

As with words, so with numbers. Various studies over recent years have revealed that, on average, people think the UK hosts 23 per cent of the world's refugees (the actual figure is unknown but considerably lower than 23 per cent)[4], and that asylum seekers receive £113 a week in benefits (the actual figure is around £37);[5] while 45 per cent of people think asylum seekers come to Britain 'because they want to live off social security payments', and 64 per cent because 'they think Britain is a "soft touch"'.[6]

Anti-asylum rhetoric may be partly responsible for this level of ignorance, but the alternative, of systematically downplaying the seriousness of the issue, is hardly more helpful. The fact is that the recent upsurge in asylum applications to the UK is totally unprecedented. During the 1980s, the average number of applications for asylum was about 5,000 a year. This rose to 35,000 between 1990 and 1997 and then to nearly 70,000 between 1998 and 2003.[7] The fact that the number of applications fell by 41 per cent in 2003 should not disguise the scale of the issue.

To get a proper understanding of the UK situation, one needs to make international comparisons. According to the United Nations High Commissioner for Refugees, there are currently around 12 million refugees worldwide, approximately 600,000 of whom have made asylum applications in industrialized nations. In the early years of the millennium, the UK received more applications than any other industrialized nation, though in terms of numbers received per 1,000 population it came 11th and in terms of wealth (i.e. applications received per US$1m Gross Domestic Product (GDP)) it came 12th.[8] The rise in UK asylum applications may be severe and unprecedented, but it is not unique.

What, then, are the factors behind this upsurge in asylum applications? A study conducted by the Institute for Public Policy Research (IPPR) that examined the causes and patterns of forced migration to the EU between 1990 and 2000 showed that, within the 20 countries that accounted for three-quarters of all asylum applications, there were eight potential 'push factors', of which the first four were dominant.[9]

1 Repression and/or discrimination of minorities, ethnic conflict and human-rights abuse
2 Civil war
3 Number of internally displaced persons (IDPs) in total population
4 Poverty
5 Position on the Human Development Index (HDI)
6 Life expectancy
7 Population density
8 Adult illiteracy rate

This analysis corresponds with the provenance of most recent UK asylum applicants: Iraq, Zimbabwe, Afghanistan, Somalia, China, Sri Lanka and Turkey are all countries which have suffered some form of conflict, repression or discrimination. Quite apart from anything else, the predominance of brutal 'push factors' makes intuitive sense. As one 17-year-old Afghani woman said to the Churches' Commission on Racial Justice in their report *Asylum Voices*, 'no one would like to leave their lifelong friends'.[10]

Such push factors do not invalidate the existence of other, 'pull' factors, however. While there is little evidence of asylum applicants shopping around for benefits, the IPPR research also cited a range of 'pull factors' to the EU, including a high level of peace and public order, democratic institutions and the rule of law, economic security, and welfare and health systems. In addition to these, issues such as geographic proximity, natural historical or cultural links, post-colonial connections, a common language, and the existence of diaspora communities all play a role in causing potential asylum seekers to prioritize one destination over another.

The obvious size, internationality and complexity of the issue and the factors that drive it make a domestic political 'solution' extremely difficult. International co-operation, through preventative diplomacy, early warning systems, effective rapid reaction and humanitarian intervention, is imperative. Ultimately domestic asylum policy can only ever be a band-aid, dealing with the painful effects of causes that lie elsewhere.

Yet, as the much-publicized fall in asylum applications in 2003–4 shows, domestic policy can have an impact. Government and opposition parties are rightly judged on their asylum record and/or policies, and if elections are to be decided on meaningful policy issues rather than personality traits or party loyalty, it is important to have an idea of what a Christian perspective on asylum might offer.

Loving the alien*

Such a perspective must be careful to avoid the pitfalls of anachronism. Biblical teaching does not speak of asylum seekers, immigrants or even refugees in the modern sense of the words. A world without defined states, secure borders and formalized human rights could have no conception of asylum application and we do the Old and New Testaments a disservice by forcing them into inappropriate categories.

The biblical narrative is, however, profoundly interested in the 'alien', 'sojourner', 'foreigner' or 'stranger', as the Hebrew word *ger* is variously translated. Israel existed at a geographical and political crossroads in the ancient Near East and had to deal with foreigners, in the form of individuals, tribes and empires, from its earliest days. An important but often overlooked verse in Exodus strongly suggests that foreigners made up a significant element of Israel's population from the time of the exodus itself.[11]

Israel's own identity was tied to that of the 'immigrant' even from the time of the Patriarchs. Abraham was called out of Ur and lived as 'an alien and a stranger' among the Hittites.[12] Israel was con-

---

* I am grateful to Dr Jonathan Burnside for his study *The Status and Welfare of the Immigrant in Old Testament Law* (Cambridge: Jubilee Centre, 2001), from which much of the material in this section is drawn.

ceived as a nation while the people were living as foreigners in Egypt. Their escape from captivity forged and fixed their identity in a way they were never allowed to forget: 'you yourselves know how it feels to be aliens, because you were aliens in Egypt'; 'Love [the alien] as yourself, for you were aliens in Egypt'; 'you shall declare before the LORD your God: "My father was a wandering Aramean"'; 'We are aliens and strangers in your sight, as were all our forefathers.'[13]

It is hardly surprising, therefore, that the *ger* is a major figure in the Old Testament. *Gerim* (the plural of *ger*) are commonly mentioned alongside hired hands, the poor, widows and orphans, implying their vulnerability and economic dependence. They are to be 'treated as one of your native-born [and] love[d] as yourself'.[14] They had equal rights to justice and were to be protected from abuse, oppression, economic exploitation and unfair treatment in the courts.[15] They also had the rights to the gleanings of the harvest, to fair employment practice, to the cities of refuge, to the triennial tithe and latterly even to rural land.[16] Condemnation of their mistreatment forms a major part of the prophets' complaints.[17]

More significantly, *gerim* were included in the feasts and practices central to Israel's identity. Providing they were prepared to make a personal sign of commitment to the covenant with God through circumcision, they were to be included in the Passover and the festivals of Weeks and Tabernacles. Inclusion in such intimate and important national festivals is remarkable, especially given Israel's geo-political vulnerability and its commitment to a distinctive exclusivity in so many areas of life.

With such 'rights' came responsibilities. The employer's duty not to force the *ger* to work on the Sabbath was as much the *ger*'s responsibility to obey the fourth commandment. In a similar way, *gerim* were to be treated equally in matters of inadvertent and defiant sin, blasphemy, murder, disfigurement and the killing of animals, and were under the same stipulation to 'keep [. . .] statutes and [. . .] ordinances'.[18] Social integration was a two-edged sword.

Not all 'aliens' were *gerim*. *Nokrim*, translated variously as 'foreigners' or 'temporary residents', were a more obviously 'foreign' element in the nation, their presence temporary, their loyalties elsewhere and their level of integration significantly lower. As far as it is possible to tell, they appear to have been consciously foreign, autonomous and independent individuals, who had little desire and, therefore, right to 'join' Israel. Their 'rights' were more limited than those of the *gerim* and their involvement in the community more circumscribed.[19] More distant still were foreign people groups, such as the Ammonites, Moabites and Edomites, who tended to be referred to as groups rather than individuals and treated with greater caution still. Overall, Israel appeared to exercise (at least in theory) a nuanced and differentiated response to 'aliens' according to their vulnerability, socio-economic status and willingness to integrate into the community.

The Old Testament's concern for the *ger* comes into particular focus in Christ's life and ministry. In much the same way as the alien, orphan and widow were grouped and recognized as the vulnerable section of Israelite society in the Torah, so Samaritans and 'strangers' were used by Christ to emphasize the call to serve those who are geographically or ethnically alien, most notably in the parable of the good Samaritan in Luke chapter 10 and in Christ's moving words in Matthew chapter 25:

> Then the righteous will answer him, "Lord [. . .] when did we see you a stranger and invite you in, or needing clothes and clothe you?" [. . .] The King will reply, "I tell you the truth, whatever you did for one of the least of these brothers of mine, you did for me."[20]

Luke's writings in particular use Samaritans to expose and accuse the wickedness of elevating ethnic prejudice over compassion. Of the ten lepers healed in Luke chapter 17, the only one who returned to thank Christ was a Samaritan (a fact which Luke is careful to point out).[21] Christ rebuked James and John in Luke chapter 9 for wanting to call down fire upon a Samaritan village that did not welcome them.[22] He commanded the disciples in Acts chapter 1 to 'be my witnesses in Jerusalem, and in all Judea and Samaria'.[23] Luke then proceeds to highlight the success of Philip's mission in Samaria after the first wave of persecution, and later on describes how Paul and Barnabas heard about the success of the Church in Samaria and reported it to the council of Jerusalem.[24] The then-contemporary interpretation of the Torah's command to love the *ger* – i.e. that the *ger* excluded Samaritans and non-resident foreigners – is systematically addressed in Luke–Acts.

Just as the Torah's call to 'love the alien' was translated into the age of the new covenant in this way, so Israel's conscious identification with the alien was also picked up by the early Church, as Peter makes clear in the introduction to his first epistle: 'Peter, an apostle of Jesus Christ, to God's elect, strangers in the world, scattered throughout Pontus, Galatia [. . .] live your lives as strangers here in reverent fear [. . .] as aliens and strangers in the world [. . .] abstain from sinful desires'.[25]

At the same time as loving aliens and identifying with them, Israel was passionately concerned to preserve its own particular identity through the festivals, symbols, practices, Temple, and stories which embodied its core beliefs, and this concern was adopted by the early Church, whose natural boundaries were to be seen in baptism, Eucharist and agape meals, modified Sabbath observance and a demanding ethical code. In welcoming the stranger as they were commanded to do, neither Israel nor the nascent Church allowed this openness to dilute their core values or identity (see Chapter 3).

The extensive prophetic critique of Israel, and some of Paul's more troubled letters, show that neither nation nor Church ever got it wholly right. Nevertheless, the underlying idea remained steadfast: loving the alien was imperative but was not a substitute for loving one's own weak and economically vulnerable, nor a means of abandoning community identity by the back door.

Morality and efficiency

Asylum policy is, by its nature, highly reactive and thus does not feature heavily in party manifestos. It is also a 'negative' social issue in that public interest tends to be motivated by fear of the worst scenario (swamping, flooding, exploitation) rather than by hope for the best (cohesion, integration, diversity). Any serious Christian engagement with the issue must take these facts into account and offer a positive vision of asylum as well as trying to address specific policies.

The first element of that vision must be to counter the hyperbole, caricature and 'tough rhetoric' that dog the debate. The issue's subtleties and sensitivity demand a tone of moderation and understanding from all involved. The counsel of perfection that some political interviewers and opposition spokesmen assume is unhelpful: there is no easy panacea, and pretending otherwise and then lambasting ministers for their 'least-worst solutions' merely serve to erode confidence in politics. At the same time, ministers need the courage to admit the fallibility, inefficiency and weakness of policy initiatives. If one thing breeds cynicism faster than an interviewer's unreasonable counsel of perfection, it is an interviewee's unreasonable claim for perfection.

Second, the insistent and repeated emphasis on loving the alien throughout the entire biblical narrative warns us that the moral imperative of welcoming the vulnerable must be our guiding light. It is better to err on the side of generosity and risk exploitation by the unscrupulous than to err on the side of inflexibility and risk the further dehumanization of the weak and vulnerable.

'Generosity' is not the same thing as laxity, however, and loving the vulnerable alien entails serious legal, financial and practical responsibilities for society. Any system that allows asylum seekers to fall into the kind of crime-ridden underworld portrayed in Stephen Frear's film *Dirty Pretty Things* is guilty of the same failure as that for which the prophets criticized Israel. Precisely how this efficient and effective reception-and-processing network is achieved will be a matter for debate, but it may demand authoritarian measures such as compulsory accommodation centres, and insistence on immediate application or the curtailment of the appeals process, depending on whether convincing research and trial periods have shown them to be beneficial.[26]

Third, and conversely, the biblical recognition of the *ger's* responsibilities and the emphasis on the importance of community cohesion remind us that asylum is a two-way process. Weakness and vulnerability do not constitute an excuse for anti-social behaviour. The willing identification of the alien with his or her host culture that is central to the biblical vision of 'asylum' needs to be reflected today. Exactly how that is achieved is, again, debatable, but it could involve compulsory lessons in English language and culture, an official, legal welcoming ceremony as part of the naturalization process, and the introduction of ID cards, although this last measure would be unacceptably divisive if restricted to any one section of the population.

Above all, it is important to articulate a positive vision of asylum. All too often, the major reason for asylum offered by those who oppose tabloid rhetoric is its economic benefit.[27] Quite apart from the fact that this argument is questionable, it is profoundly non-Christian: asylum seekers should be embraced not for their economic potential but for their human need. How we treat others is fundamental to who we are, and how we treat vulnerable others is particularly so. A nation that willingly accepts those who are fleeing from a genuine risk of persecution should be proud that it does so and does not need to excuse it with arguments of self-interest. The privatization of morality in the modern West may have made it difficult to base political decisions on moral arguments like these, but if there were ever a need for this to be reversed, it is here.

Ultimately, because domestic asylum policy is so embedded in and inextricably linked to broader international concerns, no government will be able to deliver the perfect 'solution' and voters should not expect them to. That is not to say that the government should not be judged on the success of its asylum policy, but rather to suggest that the tone of its (and other parties') rhetoric and the nature of their vision are just as important. An efficient, well-ordered and humane system is critical, but so is a vision that emphasizes the humanity and need of asylum seekers, that acknowledges the moral imperative of treating them accordingly, and that insists on their responsibility to society just as much as on society's responsibility to them.

Further engaging

Publications

Jonathan Burnside, *The Status and Welfare of the Immigrant in Old Testament Law* (Cambridge: Jubilee Centre, 2001)

Nick Spencer, *Asylum and Immigration: A Christian Perspective on a Polarized Debate* (Carlisle: Paternoster, 2004)

Websites

Churches' Commission on Racial Justice (CCRJ):
www.ctbi.org.uk/ccrj/about.htm>

City Life Education and Action for Refugees (CLEAR):
<www.clearproject.co.uk>

Enabling Christians in Serving Refugees (ECSR):
<www.ecsr.org.uk>

❸ Race and Nationhood

The issue of asylum is closely and sometimes confusingly linked to those of race and nationhood in the public's mind. The re-emergence of the far right as a serious force in continental politics over recent years has blurred the boundary between issues further. France, Austria, Denmark, Italy, Switzerland and the Netherlands have each seen political parties campaign and win seats with explicitly racist rhetoric, in which the increase in asylum applications has been used to provoke fears about people of a different 'race'.

The comparative insignificance of the British National Party is little cause for celebration. Post-war immigration to the UK exposed a latent racism in many Britons, with Afro-Caribbean, Pakistani and Bangladeshi immigrants inheriting the baton of discrimination from earlier Irish immigrants. From the riots in Nottingham and North Kensington in 1958 to the murder of Stephen Lawrence in 1993, post-war Britain has many milestones marking its painful history of race relations.[1]

Recent years have witnessed a sometimes frenzied interest in ethnicity, with the expression 'institutionally racist', defined and popularized by the Macpherson Inquiry, becoming the phrase of choice for confessions and accusations alike. Like the people of Salem, determined to eradicate witchcraft yet finding themselves haunted by it at every juncture, the British, in their eagerness to root out racism, have unearthed it everywhere.[2]

Racial prejudice is extremely difficult to measure accurately. Research is hindered by the subjectivity and sensitivity of the issue: Who defines what is prejudice and who openly calls themselves racist? According to the National Centre for Social Research, the British are (or at least *say* they are) less racially prejudiced today than they have ever been, with 67 per cent claiming they are 'not prejudiced at all'.[3] According to *The Voice of Britain*, a survey conducted for the Commission for Racial Equality

(CRE), the vast majority (86 per cent) of the British public does not believe you have to be white to be 'truly British' and more than half (59 per cent) say that Britain has good race relations between different ethnic minorities.[4]

Yet there remains a deep sense of unease. 'Race' is still very much a live issue. According to MORI's monthly political monitor, 'race relations/immigration' is now considered one of the most important issues facing the UK today (it was a long way behind health, crime, Europe and the economy in 2001).[5] In spring 2002, the unemployment rate for all minority ethnic groups was 10.7 per cent, more than double that of white adults.[6] Working-age people of Black African ethnicity were (in autumn 2003) more than twice as likely to live in workless households than white men and women of the same age.[7] People (of all ethnic groups) habitually overestimate the size of the UK's immigrant and non-white population.[8] Britain is not at ease with itself over the issue of race.

Yet if it is anxious about race, it is anxious and confused about nationhood. The four historic pillars of Britishness – union, empire, monarchy and Protestantism – so central to national identity for so long, have been severely eroded in the last half-century and there is little consensus over what should replace them, or whether Britishness should simply be permitted to devolve into its constituent elements, which, as far as the English are concerned, would solve little. The large-scale immigration of the post-war period must be seen in the context of these changes: while it may have acted as a catalyst for cultural re-evaluation, it did not cause it. Unfortunately, the concurrence of the two phenomena has led to their confusion in many quarters. Parts of the conservative right have historically blamed ethnic minorities for changing Britain, while parts of the liberal left have rejected any move towards cultural solidarity on the grounds that it is racist.

The situation is further complicated by globalization, the threat of terrorism and the existence of a welfare state. As capital flows across national borders with ever greater ease, people follow. The question of the state to which they owe their loyalty, pay their taxes and present their needs becomes very difficult. Similarly, the very existence of the nation state and the degree and type of commitment it can demand from its citizens and subjects becomes questionable, prompting some commentators to talk about new models of nationhood altogether.[9]

These issues were never far from the headlines during Labour's second term. In summer 2001, riots in Bradford, Oldham and Burnley precipitated a series of reports exploring the reasons for the violence and the lack of community cohesion in those areas. One of these commented that 'whilst respect for different cultures is vital, it will also be essential to agree some common elements of "nationhood"'. It recommended that

a meaningful concept of 'citizenship' needs establishing – and championing – which recognizes [. . .] the contribution of all cultures to this Nation's development [. . .] but establishes a clear primary loyalty to this Nation [. . . and that] a clearer statement of allegiance, perhaps along the lines of the Canadian model, should be considered.[10]

Two years later, 16 Britons gathered in Brent Town Hall and became the first to swear an oath of allegiance to Queen and country as part of the new British citizenship ceremony.

Between these two events, the attacks of September 11th, 2001, provoked many more questions about the balance between religious, cultural and national loyalties, prompting the late political commentator Hugo Young to write: 'Liberalism is betrayed by [. . .] people who put the comfort of immigrant minorities before the insistence on an irreducible list of British civic values: democracy, mutual tolerance, equality of liberty, the rule of law.'[11]

The balance between diversity and integration (or diversity and unity, or diversity and cohesion – all three phrases are popular) is a difficult one to strike. Changes in British ethnicity and culture over the last 60 years have made it particularly pressing. Whether it is to remove the stain of overtly racist politics, to calm the nation's troubled conscience, to clarify its cultural confusion, to maintain its security or to address positively the ethnic imbalances that clearly remain, race and nationhood need to be recognized as major political issues.

One race, many nations

The biblical understanding of race is grounded in Genesis chapter 1. The interesting and endlessly debated question of what 'his own image' actually means often obscures the fact that Genesis 1.26 implies that as *all* human beings come from one man (or one couple) and as that man (or couple) is made in God's image, *all* human beings bear God's image. As the Churches' Commission for Racial Justice remarks, 'There is only one race: the human race.'

Unity is not the same as uniformity, however, a fact made clear at three seminal moments in the biblical story. In the first, the universal vision of Genesis chapters 1—3 narrows down to the particular call of Abraham in Genesis chapter 12. As Jonathan Sacks writes: 'God, the creator of humanity [. . .] turns to one people and commands it to be different, teaching humanity to make space for difference. God may at times be found in human other, the one not like us'.[12] The universal picture is not lost, as God's promise 'to [bless] all peoples on earth [. . .] through [Abraham]' reminds us, but a decisive move from the archetype to the particular has been made.

Pentecost, the second moment, often cited as the New Testament's reversal of Babel, sustains rather than abolishes difference. As Luke makes clear, the linguistic diversity of the Parthians, Medes and others was not eliminated and replaced by 'one tongue' but merely and temporarily overcome. Diversity is transcended, not eradicated. In the same way, Paul later asserts that he was an 'Israelite [. . .] a descendant of Abraham, from the tribe of Benjamin', and 'a Roman citizen', while at the same time acknowledging that in Christ 'there is no Greek or Jew, circumcised or uncircumcised, barbarian [or] Scythian'.[13]

Finally, in Revelation, John uses the four-fold formula from Genesis chapter 10 – families, languages, lands, and nations – to describe the gathered people of his vision. Those who stand before the throne at the end of time have not, it appears, lost their unique, personal identities. The multitude may be countless but it is not characterless.[14]

These three vignettes point towards the biblical vision of nationhood that is most clearly seen in the only nation in which the narrative is interested in any detail, Israel itself. Nationality is not simply a matter of territory or even birth but of willing association: to be an Israelite was not primarily a question of ethnicity but one of association.[15] Whereas Roman citizenship primarily exempted one from degrading punishment and gave the right to a public trial, to be an Israelite was to identify oneself with a particular people, culture and world-view.[16]

To be an Israelite was to embrace certain key beliefs such monotheism, creation, election, covenant and redemption. It was to retell them through a series of stories, such as those of Abraham and election, Moses and liberation, David and kingship. It was to enact them in the yearly round of celebrations and festivals that united foundational moments in Israel's history with agricultural harvests. It was to embody them in symbols that shaped the Israelite mind, landscape and life: Temple, Torah, Sabbath, Jubilee, circumcision, food laws. And it was to live a distinct, moral life that would be a light to other nations, 'who will hear about all these decrees and say, "Surely this great nation is a wise and understanding people"'.[17] To be an Israelite was to make a statement of belonging, participation and values.

This outlook was, of course, vulnerable to the kind of aggressive nationalism that formed a backdrop to Christ's ministry. Centuries of occupation and persecution had bred resentment, and cultural and ethnic borders had hardened into bitter, belligerently policed fault lines. Time and again, Christ's example and stories transcended national and ethnic boundaries, and earned him condemnation. Yet his kingdom, as he told his disciples, was 'from another place' and he refused to bow to nationalist pressure.[18]

Those disciples became the quorum of his new narrative community, a people that told a new story about themselves, the world and God's relationship with both, whose boundaries were ethical, credal and baptismal. The new kingdom was to be an international 'nation', a phrase that sounds odd until one surrenders territorial or ethnic concepts of nationhood. Peter described the churches to whom he wrote as 'a holy nation'.[19] Paul told the Philippians that their citizenship was in heaven.[20] The book of Hebrews describes the examples of faith as 'aliens and strangers on earth' who were 'looking for a country of their own [. . .] a better country – a heavenly one'.[21] And Revelation has the city of New Jerusalem indicating the believers' true citizenship.[22]

This new nationality took precedence over all other identities: whoever or wherever one was, it was being 'in Christ' that mattered. Yet being in Christ did not abolish all other identities. Paul makes it clear that Jews and Greeks remained Jews and Greeks, and men and women stayed men and women. Such differences were simply now gathered into the body of the Messiah, to function in harmony to the honour of the risen Christ.

Cohesion with diversity

Christianity has a bad record over nationhood. Protestant nations have liked to view themselves as the 'new Israel'. Orthodox churches have commonly hitched their creed and culture to the wagon of ethnic nationalism, despite the condemnation of this 'phyletism' by an Orthodox council in 1872.[23] To be English was once to be Anglican.

Yet the principles outlined above – that humanity is unified but not uniform, that all people bear (and mar) God's image, that nationality is less a function of geography or ethnicity than of willing association, that nationhood demands narration, that any national boundary is liable to harden into a frontier, and that faith in Christ trumps all other loyalties – can help Christians engage meaningfully and distinctively in this sensitive debate, and offer criteria against which we can judge political statements on race and nationhood.

First, and obviously, we must apply the principle of 'one race'. This will mean rejecting all policy and rhetoric based on racial difference. It will mean wholehearted support of racial equality and the correction of public misinformation, such as the UK's perceived non-white population size, which is thought, on average, to be around one in five when the correct answer is approximately one in twelve.[24] It will also entail the need to explain and address the ethnic anomalies outlined above: why, for example, do levels of education and employment differ so greatly between certain ethnic groups?

This will not, it should be emphasized, necessitate social engineering along ethnic lines. If, for example, research shows that educational success is correlated to English-language proficiency and family stability, and that these factors happen to correlate vaguely to ethnicity (hence giving the impression that education correlates to ethnicity), the solution is not to set ethnicity quotas for educational establishments but to encourage English-language training and family stability.

At the same time, remaining with the 'one race' principle and recognizing that just as all people are marked with God's image, all have marred it, we must guard against the tendency to witch-hunt. Prejudice is not the prerogative of other people. Revulsion towards racist politics should discourage rather than sanction our use of the term 'racist'. It is such a serious accusation that we would do well to check for the dust in our own eye first. When a serious and respected thinker replies to an intelligent essay on the balance between solidarity and diversity with the words, 'Is this the wit and wisdom of Enoch Powell? Jottings from the BNP leader's weblog?' nobody benefits.[25]

Second, and in contrast to some strains of liberal individualism and multicultural thinking, we should acknowledge the reality of nationhood. Human beings are relational animals and gathered communities are genuine entities, with those, like Britain, that have long-established identities and extensive welfare systems being all the more 'real'. The desire to protect borders and safeguard distinctive characteristics should not be dismissed simply as divisive nationalism.

This is not, of course, the same as saying that modern nations must be preserved at all costs or that borders are immutable or impermeable. Borders and communities change with circumstance. 'In a world littered with the wrecks of civilisations and empire, there is nothing particularly immortal about Great Britain or any other Western nation.'[26] It is, however, to recognize the right of a nation to exist and to shape its destiny. Nations may be historically contingent but that does not mean they are immaterial.

Third, Israel's model of nationhood has several implications. It encourages a definition of belonging to the nation state that is independent of ethnicity. This, of course, is already the case in the UK, but until recently the absence of any meaningful concept of citizenship meant that while ethnicity meant nothing, neither did belonging. The introduction of citizenship ceremonies is to be welcomed, although with the warning that demanding that immigrants swear an oath of allegiance that native-born people do not, and perhaps would not, risks being divisive.

Balancing this call for citizenship is the recognition that citizenship should not demand wholesale integration. When a second-generation immigrant can make a remark like this, Christians will sympathize:

My parents' generation were completely uncritical of Great Britain [. . .] People like me are the opposite because we have grown up here [. . .] I see them drowning in drugs, divorce and depression. I see them unable to control their children. I see them producing filth and violence and claiming it is some kind of freedom. I see love between men and women evaporating [. . .] Why should I take this road in the name of progress?[27]

Citizenship does not demand an uncritical adoption of a culture's values, but rather an embrace of salient, cohesive factors: spoken and written English, a grasp of national history, society, values and civic structures. Nor is it a one-way process. The nation needs to develop points of solidarity, for example an on-going social and cultural commission and exhibition, a British national holiday or a State of the Nation address that could help foster this sense of identity. Similarly, if the nation requires immigrants to swear an oath of allegiance, perhaps it needs to codify and declare its responsibilities to its new citizens as part of the same ceremony.

Fourth, and more controversially, there is good argument for a graduated concept of citizenship, provided that citizenship obligations apply to British-born individuals too. Membership of early Israel was not compulsory for immigrants. Refusal to integrate was no bar to basic 'rights', but it is also constituted a statement that the immigrant did not wish to belong fully and so deselected him or her from full community participation. This principle points in the direction of a graduated welfare policy, such as already exists to some extent in the UK and is developing in Denmark.[28] It is a principle that sits uncomfortably with some popular notions of liberal individualism but appears to be in step with public opinion. The CRE report, *The Voice of Britain*, mentioned earlier, reported that 69 per cent of the British population thought ethnic minorities needed 'to demonstrate a real commitment before they can be considered British' (although this displays a regrettable confusion between ethnicity and immigration). It must be emphasized that this is not an excuse to abuse or dehumanize those who refuse citizenship: both the Torah and Christ explicitly reject such behaviour. It is, however, to recognize that any nation that wishes to maintain a meaningful welfare state must also maintain the sense of cohesion and solidarity that makes it possible.[29]

The issues of race and nationhood are so sensitive that they are often smothered under anodyne language or ignored altogether at election time. Yet they are central to the most basic questions of life today and should not be ignored. The Christian vision of community cohesion with diversity will not 'solve' the various problems that trouble politicians, but remains a useful one against which political pronouncements may be judged.

Further engaging

Publications

Yasmin Alibhai-Brown, *Who Do We Think We Are?* (London: Penguin, 2000)

J. Daniel Hays, *From Every People and Nation: A Biblical Theology of Race* (Downers Grove: IVP, 2003)

Peter Hitchens, *The Abolition of Britain* (London: Quartet Books, 1999)

Julian Rivers, *Multiculturalism* (Cambridge Papers, Vol. 10, No. 4, December 2001)

Richard Weight, *Patriots: National Identity in Britain 1940–2000* (London: Macmillan, 2002)

Websites

Commission for Racial Equality: <www.cre.gov.uk>

Institute for Citizenship: <www.citizen.org.uk>

❹ International Order

The events of September 11th, 2001 transformed Labour's second term in power. The government's ten election manifesto goals were temporarily overshadowed as Samuel Huntington's predicted 'clash of civilizations' shocked the world and international security became the issue of the moment.[1]

The almost immediate US-led response against the Taliban in Afghanistan involved NATO in war and the United Nations in peace, hence broadening the question of international security into one of international legitimacy. When America turned its gaze on Iraq that question attained painful urgency. The tension between America's willingness to use military power in pursuit of international security (and, its critics would say, of its economic interests) and the alternative of a 'world of laws and rules and transnational negotiation and cooperation', sometimes labelled as the European approach (which its critics accuse of decision-making paralysis), was all too evident.[2]

While all this was happening, the 'European project' was gathering pace. Euro notes were introduced in 2002, followed by the Treaty of Nice, the Union's expansion into eastern Europe, and the (initially aborted) completion of a draft constitution. Having slipped down the political agenda during Labour's first term, 'Europe' was back, bringing with it questions about the continued role of the sovereign nation state. While some claimed the European constitution was 'a mere tidying-up exercise', others, not least some prominent European politicians, openly described it as a key step on the path towards a single European state. In the words of Romano Prodi: 'The single market was the theme of the Eighties; the single currency was the theme of the Nineties; we must now face the difficult task of moving towards a single economy, a single political unity.'[3]

The British public's fear of losing national sovereignty propelled the UK Independence Party to its best results in the 2004

European elections and highlighted the (for some, artificial) choice between international integration and national isolation.

In the background to these trends and to some extent driving them was the issue of globalization.[4] Although often used in different ways, the term 'globalization' is widely understood to refer to the emergence of a single, global economy, in which historical barriers to free trade have been removed, and capital and other resources cross national borders without hindrance. This economic trend is the engine for others, such as cultural globalization (which often means Americanization) and the emergence of international political power blocs and, ultimately, global government. Roman Herzog, then German President, expressed the implications of economic globalization well in a speech to the World Economic Forum in Davos in 1999:

> If [. . .] capital and investment focus too much on chasing [. . .] prices around the world, what, if anything, is left for politics, society and culture? [. . .] Will politics degenerate into a mere repair shop for economic developments which are damaging in human or social terms? If this were the case, globality [i.e. the end result of globalization] would have robbed politics of its essence: its orientation towards people [. . .] Globality forces us to seek not only a new economic and financial order, but also a worldwide social order.[5]

The implications of this for the sovereign nation state are enormous. At its most extreme, in Herzog's own words, 'the day of the nation state is over'.[6] Less apocalyptically, the British diplomat Robert Cooper has talked about the development of the 'postmodern state', in which historic sovereign states remain important but become transparent, interdependent and open to 'mutual interference'.[7] Alternatively, the American historian and strategist Philip Bobbitt has written about the emergence of the 'market state', in which 'the function of government [. . .] is to clear a space for individuals or groups to do their own negotiating, to secure the best deal or the best value for money in pursuing what they want'.[8]

However the international order develops in the twenty-first century, there is bound to be tension: between nation states and international power structures; between national sovereignty and international law; between interventionist and isolationist approaches to international problems; between idealism and pragmatism. The manner in which these tensions are resolved will shape the identity, security and opportunities of billions of people.

Multipolarity and subsidiarity

One should not expect to find unambiguous answers to such detailed and specific questions in biblical teaching. Not only are our concepts of international order and legislation anachronistic, but the biblical narrative itself encompasses centuries of political change. As the theologian Chris Wright has written, the Bible offers 'no single "doctrine of the state", but a variety of responses to an ever-changing human institution', a fact that should warn us against elaborating a prescriptive or inflexible model for the modern world order.[9]

That said, the biblical understanding of the role of government and its use in later Christian teaching can be used to guide and inform our vision of the international order. The political structure outlined in the Torah was multipolar, encompassing six independent sources of authority, each with its own jurisdiction.[10] These were the individual, the family, the community, the Levites, the tribe or region, and the nation. Between them they formed a network of concurrent authorities each instituted by God and protected, limited and empowered by the national constitution. The six areas could overlap and were non-hierarchical, so that the 'small' was not automatically subservient to the 'large'. Marriage, for example, took precedence over military service for a year, and the king was subject to the law, as preserved and taught by the Levites.[11]

As far as possible, this multipolar political structure, which reflected the diverse nature of society, made government an immediate and concrete fact of life, rather than a distant, abstract entity. Its combination of a respect for the natural ties of family, community and locality and legislation for wider authorities was intended to safeguard individual worth and ensure social integration, while maintaining the flexibility to address larger problems.

The depiction of empire in both Testaments is, accordingly, often hostile, not entirely surprisingly, given Israel's and the early Church's experience of Egypt, Assyria, Babylonia and Rome. Amos, Isaiah, Jeremiah, Daniel and Ezekiel all condemned their leaders for political imperialism and Cyrus of Persia is the only imperial figure judged in any way positively.[12] Instead, in the same way as God and Samuel are reluctant to elect a king over Israel for fear of the consequences of such centralization, the biblical narrative insists that Christ alone is the sole ruler of the nations. Worldwide government is dangerous: too distant from the concerns of the individual and too close to God's unique authority. Only the Church has truly international reach and sanction, and that is as an organ of witness, not government.

The development of Hebraic studies during the Reformation saw some of these ideas utilized in the emerging covenantal approach to politics.[13] In opposition to, for example, Thomas Hobbes' vision of a strong, authoritarian state that would resist the otherwise 'solitary, poor, nasty, brutish and short' nature of life, 'covenant theologians understood the whole community to be fundamentally bound to God as creator and thence to one another'.[14] Their conception of the people standing directly under the sovereignty of God in covenant relationship, combined with an emphasis upon the priesthood of all believers, led them to prioritize a diversity in the range of social institutions over calls for political centralization.

This approach was further developed by the Dutch theologian and statesman, Abraham Kuyper, who advanced the idea of sphere-sovereignty. This asserted that the state was not the source of legitimacy for, and did not have sovereignty over, other spheres, such as business, family, church, or educational establishments. The social order is naturally and properly pluriform, its diverse institutions relate to one another on the basis of their particular character, and God alone has ultimate sovereignty.

The Roman Catholic concept of subsidiarity shares many features of this Reformed, covenantal thinking. The principle of subsidiarity as articulated in a Papal encyclical of 1931 states that 'it is an injustice [. . .] and disturbance of right order to assign to a greater and higher association what lesser and subordinate organizations can do'.[15] Subsidiarity shares an emphasis on God's sovereignty and the consequent social decentralization, and is equally concerned to protect the mediating structures between God and the individual so critical to the health of civil society.

The idea of subsidiarity was refined in later Catholic teaching and adopted as a principle within the (then) European Community, with the Maastricht Treaty 'resolv[ing] to continue the process of creating an ever closer union among the peoples of Europe, in which decisions are taken as closely as possible to the citizen in accordance with the principle of subsidiarity'.[16] This international application of the principle has not, of course, answered all the questions about international legitimacy. On the one hand there is the question of whether subsidiarity is, in fact, applied in any meaningful way within the European Union. On the other, there is the question of what decentralized authority can actually achieve. Roman Herzog's call for a global social and political order could, for example, been seen as a subsidiarity-driven reaction to the fact of economic globalization.

Yet, the biblical emphasis on multipolarity and covenant, and the related ideas of subsidiarity and sphere-sovereignty, do, at least, equip Christians to think through their attitudes to the international order and offer a vision in which the unconscious drift towards centralization is checked and global structures exist simply because more localized ones are demonstrably ineffective.

The moral imperative

As we have already noted, nationhood is a real and valid concept and should not be dismissed as a historically contingent irrelevance. This is not an excuse for nationalism or for international politics that seek the nation's welfare at any cost. As Archbishop William Temple remarked during the Second World War, 'when we turn to prayer it could not be as Britons who happened to be Christians; it must be as Christians who happened to be British. Otherwise we fall into the error of our enemies, whose distinctive sin it was that they put their nationality first.'[17]

It is, however, to recognize that nations, particularly democratic ones, are based on a genuine sense of 'we', and although this can and does change, it should not be ignored. As Roger Scruton has written: 'Democracies owe their existence to national loyalties [. . .] without national loyalty, opposition is a threat to government, and political disagreements create no common ground'.[18] This suggests that this issue, perhaps more than any other, needs to heed public opinion. When the fundamental questions concern where and with whom people feel they belong, people's opinion is obviously crucial. That opinion can be and, regrettably, is, manipulated by media and business interests. Nevertheless, given the importance of a sense of belonging to the overall issue of the international order, the fact that, for example, the population currently feels so much more British than European should not be taken lightly.

The ideas outlined above also advise us of the need to scrutinize and justify any moves towards centralization. This is emphatically *not* to say that all international bodies are invalid, as some conservative American Christians have suggested.[19] It is, however, to take the principles of multipolarity and subsidiarity seriously and to demand that if power is to be moved from the local and regional towards the continental and international, there need to be good reasons.

Such reasons may exist. George Monbiot has observed that

because the problems facing the world today are truly international in their scope, only international government can deal with them.[20] Virtual terrorist networks, international migration, environmental destruction, the actions of multinational corporations, the drastic economic imbalance between Western and African nations: none of these can be successfully addressed by atomized, sovereign nation states.

There is undoubtedly much truth in this analysis, although a Christian approach might stipulate that if power were to move from existing nation states, to which populations have some loyalty, to broader, international bodies, to which few have any allegiance, there needs to be good reason. Centralizing power is not necessarily a bad thing but, as God's response to Israel's demands for a king in 1 Samuel 8 reminds us, it is potentially dangerous and dehumanizing.

Irrespective of where one draws the lines of appropriate power, the all-encompassing vision of the biblical narrative counsels us to take our international responsibilities seriously and recognize the country's global moral responsibility. At election time, this stands to be a genuinely counter-cultural approach. The fact that neither the size of the overseas aid budget nor the enormous economic gap between 'the West' and (much of) 'the rest' is considered a major issue facing Britain today is understandable if not excusable. Any political vision which takes God's love of *all* seriously will view the fact that 'one billion of the world's poorest people are living without safe drinking water' as an important domestic issue, even if next to none of those people live in the UK.[21]

In his book *Is there a Gospel for the Rich?* Richard Harries, Bishop of Oxford, describes how, when lecturing on that topic, people often approached him and said, 'I must ring my wealthy friends and persuade them to come.' Harries comments: 'It was always assumed that the wealthy were other people. One of the most curious and slightly perverted features of riches is that very few people will actually admit they are rich. The rich are always other people'.[22] His words are strangely apt for Christian electoral engagement with the international order. The majority of British voters are very wealthy. We earn and own vastly more than most of the rest of the world. *We* are the rich. The manner in which national elections naturally prioritize national interests can often blind us to this fact. At best, we vote for the party whose vision of the international order best suits our national interest. At worst, we do not even think about international affairs.

Yet, the prophets' frequent judgement on Israel and her neighbours, not to mention the final vision of people from 'every tribe and language and people and nation'[23] coming together before God, reminds us that national interest is no substitute for international moral responsibility. Neither sphere-sovereignty nor subsidiarity entails international isolationism. Indeed, in the context of this broader Christian vision, they demand the opposite. If the nation seeks to preserve its sovereignty in the belief that, as it currently stands, that sovereignty is the best reflection of the collective sense of belonging, it must use it for the benefit of those in lower-income countries and not simply ignore their plight in the quest for still higher living standards. To do so would be to become the national embodiment of the rich young man of Matthew chapter 19.

Ultimately, Christians will vote for parties with more or less internationalist visions according to what they believe is the most effective way of dealing with global problems: so far, so predictable. Yet, to favour a vision of the international order that is prepared to sacrifice domestic living standards in the search for international justice and economic equity, that treats the international aid budget as a serious domestic concern, that campaigns vigorously for the abolition of crippling debt repayments – that is a counter-cultural way of engaging with the politics of the international order.

Further engaging

Publications

Philip Bobbitt, *The Shield of Achilles: War, Peace and the Course of History* (London: Allen Lane, 2002)

Robert Cooper, *The Breaking of Nations: Order and Chaos in the Twenty-First Century* (London: Atlantic Books, 2003)

Peter Heslam, *Globalization and the Good* (London: SPCK, 2004)

Peter Heslam, *Globalization: Unravelling the New Capitalism* (Cambridge: Grove Books, 2002)

Robert Kagan, *Paradise and Power* (London: Atlantic Books, 2003)

Julian Rivers, *The New World Order?* (Cambridge Papers, Vol. 8, No. 4, December 1999)

Roger Scruton, *The Need for Nations* (London: Civitas, 2004)

Websites

CAFOD: <www.cafod.org.uk>

Christian Aid: <www.christian-aid.org.uk>

Tearfund: <www.tearfund.org>

❺ Education

When, on 27 January 2004, Labour won its controversial Commons vote to allow English universities to charge variable 'top-up' fees, it suffered the largest rebellion against any government for decades. It also disregarded its 2001 manifesto pledge not to introduce such fees.

The party's willingness to break faith over this issue was an indication of how determined it was to fulfil another election promise, of seeing 50 per cent of young adults entering higher education by 2010. 'Higher education', the manifesto explained, 'brings on average 20 per cent higher earnings and a 50 per cent lower chance of unemployment'.[1] The nation could only benefit from such an expansion, even if it would not pay for it.

The government's explanation for its higher-education target unwittingly goes straight to the heart of the education debate today and raises issues that are common to all Western governments. The political questions of *who* should be educated and *how* invariably rest on the more philosophical one: *why*? What is education for?

The (albeit brief) answers offered in the 2001 manifesto, that education increases income and reduces unemployment, are both correct and reasonable. Monetary wealth and low unemployment benefit both individuals and communities, and are just objectives for education. While they might be criticized for being too utilitarian, that criticism is misplaced: education invariably has some utility. Instead, the real question lies in what that utility is. Optimizing income, marketability and productivity are reasonable but insufficient objectives, ignoring education's role in benefiting society or enabling people to appreciate life more profoundly. It is this confusion or narrowness of utility that lies at the heart of so many contentious educational issues today.

Education has, in the opinion of many, been reduced to an employability conveyer belt, whose progress is marked by a near-continuous round of tests and examinations. Few doubt the benefit or necessity of exams, but their ubiquity stands them in danger of becoming the ends rather than part of the means of education.[2] Similarly, the need to demonstrate continuous improvement has led to the perceived reduction in public-examination standards and the accusation of artificial fixing of pass rates over recent years, so that A-levels are now considered by some to be ineffective ways of adjudicating between students.[3]

The government's objective of establishing a performance culture across the public services in order to achieve these goals has, in its turn, bred a culture of targets and paperwork in the education profession. According to the Treasury's 2004 paper *Devolving Decision Making*, schools now face a total of 207 different targets, measures and 'compliance requirements'.[4] Teaching has less to do with imparting knowledge, let alone passion, and more to do with meeting centrally set testing targets, the ubiquity of which is commonly resented.

As if this were not stressful enough, 'teachers have become social workers as a result of the breakdown of the nuclear family, which has left many parents unwilling or unable to support or help their children'.[5] Reports continually show how today's teachers regularly experience abuse that would have been unthinkable 50 years ago, how poor pupil behaviour is turning lessons into 'a constant battle just to be allowed to teach', and how lack of parental support is undermining teachers' authority.[6] A number of schools have police officers stationed permanently with them and in 2003 a comprehensive school in Kent became the first to introduce random drug tests for pupils. According to a Youth Justice Board survey, around one in five pupils admit to playing truant, despite new government measures to punish parents for their children's absence.[7] Such circumstances make education much more difficult and raise the question of what it is appropriate for a school and teachers to do.

Schools' discipline problems are not, of course, simply the fault of an economically utilitarian approach to education. They do, however, point to the need for an education that develops moral values rather than one that simply fosters employability, and for an education system in which schooling is integrated into a broader social context of family and community life. Education is not an isolated phenomenon, to be shaped by market forces and consumer choice, but part of and, indeed, a microcosm of society. Schools are embodied in and need an appropriate social context, the ethos of which can have more impact on a school's culture and success than any amount of Whitehall policy. Our vision of society invariably shapes our vision of education:

This point was well articulated by Robert Reich, Professor of Social and Economic Policy at Brandeis University, in his 2004 Higher Education Policy Institute Lecture.[8] Using the example of higher education in the US as 'a cautionary tale' of how the marketization of education can result in the loss of its public mission, he warned that

> There has been a decline [in the US . . .] in the mission of public education. Instead of a public investment for a public return, instead of the rationale being to mobilise the most talented members of society for the good of society, for social leadership in a more complex world [. . .] the emphasis has shifted.

Instead, there are today two major objectives for education:

> One has to do with personal or family investment [. . .] higher education is thought to be a personal or family investment [. . .] not all that dissimilar from an investment in the stock market [. . .] The second [. . .] is that higher education should provide a possibility of upward mobility for talented individuals.

The result is that those goals in life that do not fit into this perspective are devalued:

> As you envision higher education as a system of private investment for private return and as that sinks into the public's mind,

it naturally follows that the concept of a liberal arts education or an education in humanities or the education in broad-based social sciences or in classics [. . .] has less and less justification in the public's mind.

Without a specific vision of the public good and, indeed, of individual human flourishing, education will inevitably be moulded in the image of the dominant social model. If that model is, like ours, one of being employable in order to be economically productive, the education system will be shaped accordingly, and entire areas such as humanities, morality and relationship skills may be included but will become self-conscious appendages.

The beginning of wisdom

The idea of education is central to the biblical view of the world. The word 'Torah' literally means 'instruction' or 'teaching'. Its commands were to be engraved 'upon your hearts [. . . and] impress[ed . . .] on your children'.[9]

Education was to be a '360-degree' experience, conducted 'when you sit at home and when you walk along the road, when you lie down and when you get up'.[10] This fact was reinforced by the description of Israel in Exodus 19 as 'a kingdom of priests'.[11] This, as Jonathan Sacks has pointed out, could not have been meant in a literal sense as Israel had a distinct priesthood that was confined to Aaron and his sons. Instead, in an interesting analysis that ties this passage in Israel's history with the known evolution of the modern alphabet, Sacks suggests that the phrase had a significantly different meaning: 'In most premodern societies the priesthood had one notable characteristic. Priests could read and write [. . .] Understood functionally [. . .] the phrase "a kingdom of priests" means a society of universal literacy'.[12] Whether this ideal was ever realized is doubtful (though it may be significant that Amos, for example, was a shepherd), but the fact remains that the vision for education was universal and woven into the very fabric of the nation.

The reason for or utility of this vision was encapsulated in the idea of wisdom. Variously personified as a woman, prophet, sister, teacher and counsellor,[13] wisdom offered 'long life [. . .] riches and honour'.[14] She was not simply a means to wealth, however, as she herself 'is more profitable than silver and yields better returns than gold'.[15] Her ways 'are pleasant ways, and all her paths are peace [. . .] she is a tree of life to those who embrace her'.[16]

Importantly, and in a way that was picked up in the prologue to John's Gospel, Proverbs goes on to say:

> By wisdom the LORD laid the earth's foundations,
>   by understanding he set the heavens in place;
> by his knowledge the deeps were divided,
>   and the clouds let drop the dew.[17]

This doctrine that creation was ordered, and its implication that, through the acquisition of wisdom, that order was intelligible by humans, are echoed in various different ways in the Psalms,[18] Ecclesiastes,[19] John's Gospel[20] and Romans,[21] and was seminal to the birth of modern science. The earliest signs of this mentality can be seen in Solomon's achievements as described in 1 Kings chapter 4: 'He described plant life, from the cedar of Lebanon to the hyssop that grows out of walls. He also taught about animals and birds, reptiles and fish'.[22] It is later seen in the Wisdom of Solomon,[23] but really bore fruit many centuries later when 'natural theology' developed in the West, guided by the principle that the world was God's book of works, which complemented the Bible, his book of words.[24]

It is also worth noting, in passing, that the Hebrew concept of knowing differed from later Western models, which attempted 'to locate and occupy a non-ideological vantage-point, from which reality may be surveyed and interpreted'.[25] Instead, the Hebrew idea involved a wholehearted giving of the self rather than withdrawing into a (mythical) objectivity. Knowing God demanded surrendering oneself to him, rather than objectifying him, and the same went for other people – one reason why 'knowing' someone became a euphemism for sex. The implication was that the attainment of knowledge and wisdom involved the responsibility inherent in relationship rather than the independence of supposed objectivity.

This vision of an education that is embedded within culture and led by wisdom that will 'guide [. . .] protect [. . .] exalt [. . . and] honour you'[26] is adopted in the New Testament. Christ is the supreme teacher, and his followers are called to be disciples or 'learners'. The epistles, themselves educational documents intended to inform and guide their recipients, lay out the need for 'some to be [. . .] teachers'[27] and stress the importance and utility of this education:

> Continue in what you have learned and have become convinced of, because you know those from whom you learned it [. . .] All Scripture is God-breathed and is useful for teaching, rebuking, correcting and training in righteousness, so that the man of God may be thoroughly equipped for every good work.[28]

The ultimate goal of this education, as of the Old Testament's instruction to 'meditate on the law'[29] and 'love wisdom', is to 'bear [. . .] fruit in every good work, growing in the knowledge of God'.[30]

From schooling to education

This vision for education – a universal and community-rooted process for the acquisition of wisdom, by means of which all may know God, live long and well, and celebrate life to the full – has implications for our engagement with education today. First, it sees a distinction between education and schooling. Learning is not confined to schools. Being formally taught may be an integral part of, but is not the same thing as, being educated. Teachers, conversely, cannot be expected to be official agents of social welfare or surrogate parents as well as formal educators. Families and communities need to take responsibility for schools and engage in the educational process, and schools need to be integrated into their appropriate local contexts. This may be achieved by encouraging the role of parent governors, Parent–Teacher Associations (PTAs), and parent participation and volunteering, by punishing parents for their children's truancy, or by the establishment of schools by local community groups. Legislating for this may be problematic, but treating schools as retail outlets that sell education, between which parents can choose with little personal commitment, is not satisfactory.

Second, it advises against a narrowly utilitarian vision for schools. Schooling is not simply the preparation for employment. Wisdom, rather than grades, is the objective. Although examinations play a vital role in education, their present ubiquity and supreme importance is unhelpful. Similarly, there is much to recommend lower levels of bureaucracy, fewer centrally set compliance requirements, and a willingness to devolve responsibility to local levels, although this should not entail abandoning all overarching processes for ensuring quality. The quest for educational subsidiarity should not be at the cost of an unaccountability or complacency that fails children.

There is also reason to question the determination that a certain percentage of young people should enter university-type higher education. Re-evaluating such principles will raise its own questions, such as: Are we willing to risk local inequality in pursuit of local autonomy? (see Chapter 1), or: Can we develop an attractive and positive educational path that circumvents higher education rather than one that is seen as second-best? Such questions aside, however, there is a need to move away from the heavily controlled, one-size-fits-all, conveyer-belt model of educational development.

The Christian vision is also anti-utilitarian in so far as it recommends a broad education that does not simply prioritize economics and business studies over music, art and sport in the pursuit of marketability. Matthew Arnold's attitude to culture may sound antiquated today, but it has rarely been bettered as a statement of the value of a broad, demanding but ultimately humanizing education:

> Culture [is] a pursuit of our total perfection by means of getting to know, on all the matters which most concern us, the best which has been thought and said [. . . in such a way as enables people to question their] stock notions and habits.[31]

Schooling needs to have its sights set on life rather than just work.

Third, the Christian vision places strong emphasis on 360-degree education, both in time, via lifelong learning, and space, via non-school environments that encourage active development. The role of parents in pre-school learning is vital, as are, at later stages, the uniformed organizations, sports, music and book clubs, public meetings, discussion groups and adult education courses, each of which acts as a bulwark against the ubiquitous television.

Fourth, the need to prioritize and encourage moral and relational education could not be more pressing, both inside and beyond the classroom. This should foster a sense of national identity, a meaningful concept of citizenship, democratic participation, public health, a respect for cultural diversity, and the value of cultural cohesion, as well as developing relationship skills, and qualities of sacrifice, respect and discipline. This is not to suggest that such objectives are ignored today. The preamble to the 1988 Education Reform Act states that schools must 'promote the spiritual, moral [and] cultural [. . .] development of pupils', and surveys record how pupils trust teachers highly and often rate them among their best moral educators.[32] The real need is to foster and maintain this function in the face of pressure for more obviously measurable results.

Finally, returning to the specific and vexed issue of 'top-up' fees and the government's 50 per cent higher-education target, while a Christian vision for education cannot stipulate whether they are just or not, it can offer some direction for further thinking. 'Top-up' fees should not be allowed to become a disincentive to lower-income students (hardly a controversial point). They should not be allowed to foster a vision of education as private investment, as Robert Reich warned, or to feed our debt culture, particularly among the young. And the 50 per cent higher-education target should not be allowed to lower standards in higher education and thus destroy the very reason for sending young people to university in the first place. None of these amounts to a knockdown argument one way or the other, but that is perfectly acceptable: Christians can and will legitimately disagree on policy measures while sharing the same vision and values.

Ultimately, it is the vision and values of a society that will shape its education system. A libertarian, materialist and relativist society will breed libertarian, materialist and relativist schools and students. One that is rounded, relational and guided by the principle of wisdom will focus on those goals, and although achieving them will be beyond any one government's ability, education policy can, at least, help create an infrastructure that promotes such goals.

Further engaging

Publications
Tom Bentley, *Learning Beyond the Classroom: Education for a Changing World* (London: Routledge, 1998)
Neil Postman, *The End of Education* (London: Vintage, 1996)
David Smith and John Shortt, *The Bible and the Task of Teaching* (Nottingham: Stapleford Centre, 2002)

Websites
Association of Christian Teachers: <www.christian-teachers.org.uk>
Catholic Education Service: <www.catholiceducation.org.uk>
Christian Action Research and Education: <www.care.org.uk>
Independent Schools' Christian Alliance: <www.tisca.info>
National Society: <www.natsoc.org.uk>

Stapleford Centre: <www.stapleford-centre.org>
Transforming Lives: <www.transforminglives.org.uk>

❻ Transport and Mobility

Focus groups conducted during Labour's first term in power told the government unequivocally that transport was not an important issue for the public. The 'fuel crisis' of September 2000, coupled with a sequence of rail accidents, the introduction of road congestion charging, and proposed airport expansions appeared to say otherwise. The issues may have had as much to do with taxation or the effectiveness of public–private partnerships as they did transport, but that did not save the government from critical headlines and the general perception that its transport policy was inept.

With the benefit of hindsight, however, it appears that the focus groups were correct. MORI's monthly issues poll showed that throughout this period transport lagged a long way behind health, education, foreign affairs and crime in the public's list of concerns. It was deemed one of the most important issues facing the UK today by, on average, only 10 per cent of people, compared with 45 per cent for health and 25 per cent for crime. It was only specific, short-term crises that inflated it into a major concern. The rest of the time the public was only hazily interested.

Why, then, include it as a key area for Christians to engage with? The answer is that transport is something of an 'iceberg' issue: the 'visible tenth' of sporadic transport crises hides the submerged and rather more significant long-term impact of *mobility*.

The UK's post-war economic development made possible, indeed demanded, a significant increase in personal mobility. Since 1980, rail fares have risen by 38 per cent in real terms, bus and coach fares by 33 per cent and the cost of fuel by 6 per cent.[1] Over the same period, the overall cost of motoring has fallen slightly but the average disposable income has nearly doubled. The result is that all travel, but particularly car travel, is relatively cheaper.

Not surprisingly, we travel much further and much more frequently today than at any time in the past. Since 1952 the UK has accommodated 70,000 kilometres of new road and 23 million more cars.[2] Total road traffic increased by 77 per cent between 1980 and 2002.[3] The number of passengers processed at UK airports increased from 50 million in 1980 to 168 million in 2002.[4] Globalization and our love of cheap food has resulted in goods being flown and driven millions more miles than at any time in the past: supermarket lorries cover nearly a billion kilometres a year in the UK alone.[5] We also move house more frequently than ever before (with the exception of the housing boom in the late 1980s), with around 1.5 million housing transactions per year today.[6] We have become a nation always on the move.

There is much to celebrate in all this. Mobility has afforded us freedom and opportunities only dreamt of by previous generations. We are, nevertheless, beginning to realize that when mobility becomes 'hypermobility' its social and environmental costs can outweigh its personal benefits.[7] The environmental impact of car dependency is the best-known of these costs but far from the only one. Our frenetic travelling weakens communities. Although we spend no more *time* travelling today than we did in 1952, the changing nature of travel – more time spent driving to more widely scattered friends, relatives, amenities and workplaces – has left shallower roots and a decrease in 'local interaction time'. Where we reside has increasingly little to do with where we live our lives. Neighbourhoods become more anonymous and less convivial as our weakened sense of attachment leads to civic disengagement and erodes 'social capital' or community spirit.

This, in turn, breeds crime. People are far more willing to steal from strangers and institutions than from personal acquaintances, and fluid, anonymous 'communities' afford them greater opportunity to do so. Current remedies – domestic security measures, all-pervasive surveillance technology, gated communities and private roads – are expensive and generate a siege mentality in which all public space is potentially hostile. The one exception, the neighbourhood watch scheme, ironically imitates the natural behaviour of pre-mobile communities.

'Hypermobility' is particularly hostile to children. Although far fewer children are killed on roads today than in 1922 (when there was very little traffic and a nationwide 20 mph speed limit), this is because far fewer children play outdoors. Road traffic is inimical to children's play, and anonymous societies breed a fear of 'stranger danger'. The resulting enforced lack of independence contributes to childhood obesity and impairs social development, with children's experience of mixing independently with peers and learning to cope without adult supervision being limited to the gated (and guarded) school playground.[8]

A hypermobile society is also a more socially polarized one. Mobility is strongly correlated to household car ownership, and car ownership is strongly correlated to household income. In the top fifth of incomes, half of all households have access to two or more cars, whereas in the bottom one, 71 per cent have no car. Accordingly, the average distance travelled to work by those in the highest income bracket is over eleven miles, compared with less than five miles for those in the lowest one.[9] Superficially this might sound like a good thing, with the poorest in society not suffering from the anonymity and social dislocation that hypermobility inflicts on others. However, because this group is anomalous it ends up suffering rather than benefiting. With society tailored to mobility generally and to the car specifically, those too old, young, poor, or ill to drive become second-class citizens, with a restricted choice of jobs, amenities and shops. When retailers locate out of town to accommodate the car-driving majority, the car-less minority suffer.

Finally, a hypermobile society is geographically dispersed, physically unappealing and culturally homogenized. Car dependency encourages suburban sprawl and chain-store colonization, as independent retailers are unable to compete with seven-day-a-week chain stores and the economies of scale they negotiate. The result, as Tom Wolfe described in his novel, *A Man in Full*, is that 'the only way you could tell you were leaving one community and entering another was when the franchises started repeating and you spotted another 7–Eleven, another Wendy's, another Costco'.[10]

Transport may be of only secondary public concern but it is, in reality, the 'political' tip of the much larger, 'social' iceberg of mobility. Exposing this often submerged issue shows how it, or, more precisely, our expectation of cheap, unrestricted mobility, reflects issues of community, crime, childhood, social equality and the environment. How we engage in the transport and mobility debate will indicate what we want in each of these other areas.

Rooted but not parochial

Transport, let alone our modern, individualized, day-to-day, hyper-mobile transport, was not an issue for biblical societies. The Israelites were not great seafarers and the only substantive travel we read about in either Testament was enforced.[11]

Despite this, stories of mobility and of its counterpart, rooted-ness, run through the entire biblical narrative. Humanity is settled in and then exiled from the garden of God's good creation. The agricultural Cain murders the flock-keeping Abel and is con-demned to be a 'restless wanderer', a punishment 'more than [he] can bear'.[12] Abraham is summoned from his settled life in Ur and called to travel to a distant land where he would be used to bless 'all peoples on earth'.[13] Israel's settled captivity in Egypt ends in the exodus and a lifetime of wandering. The subsequent possession of Canaan is contingent on the people's faithfulness there and is later revoked in their exile to Babylon. Christ was known for his origins yet lived a life of self-proclaimed homelessness, with 'nowhere to lay his head'.[14] Paul's ministry was to numerous locally rooted communities around the eastern Mediterranean, between which he travelled for 30 years. The vision of Revelation sees the dispersed multitude assemble before the throne of God.

This continual oscillation, in which normative rootedness is often disturbed by the upheaval of mobility, either for a higher calling or as punishment, reveals a number of principles that explain the ideas behind and the importance of both rootedness and mobility.

Being rooted and having a sense of place was recognized as a fundamental aspect of being human. Rootedness symbolized and enabled participation and belonging within the community. When Naboth refused to sell his vineyard to King Ahab in 1 Kings 21 he was not simply being bloody-minded but preserving his family stake in the community. The extensive land lists in Numbers and Joshua, the Jubilee land laws in Leviticus, and the boundary-stone regulations in Deuteronomy and Hosea further testify to the importance attached to rootedness.[15] Meaningful relationships and social justice required a common, protected and valued sense of place. Roots enabled a serious commitment to and involvement in family and community relationships, which were the foundation of welfare and social inclusion.

Practice did not always match theory, however. Naboth was killed for refusing to sell up, a crime for which Elijah condemned Ahab, and later prophets often lambasted the people for their abuse of land rights. Micah declaimed against those who 'covet fields and seize them, and houses, and take them', saying, 'They defraud a man of his home, a fellow-man of his inheritance.'[16] Amos proclaimed the time of the Lord's judgement on 'you who trample the needy and do away with the poor of the land'.[17] Isaiah's famous song of the vineyard allegorized Israel's history in Canaan through land imagery, and prophesied the nation's destruction because the owner 'looked for a crop of good grapes but it yielded only bad fruit'.[18]

The ideal of each family and community rooted in its rightful land inheritance is implicit in these prophetic criticisms, as is the potential danger of being rooted. Human nature being what it is, rootedness can breed an exclusive, insular mentality or one that treats land as simply a tradable commodity with no value beyond its market price. For this reason, the Israelites were clearly reminded in Leviticus 25 that 'the land is [God's] and you are but aliens and my tenants'.[19] The *idea* of being mobile – of the Israelites being sojourners or leaseholders in their 'own' country rather than being its inalienable freeholders – was to act as an antidote to the potential dangers of rootedness.[20]

This tension between the importance of being rooted and yet maintaining an openness to God and to others was often evident in Christ's ministry. The majority of his life was spent rooted in Nazareth, although his brief ministry was thoroughly peripatetic.[21] Those he called to leave their homes and follow him were matched by those he told to return home and give thanks.

When asked by the legal expert in Luke chapter 10, 'Who is my neighbour?' he replied with a story that cut across ethnic and cultural boundaries without losing a sense of the importance of rootedness.[22] Samaritans, as noted above, were deeply loathed and not considered among the *gerim* Israel was commanded to love. Yet, Christ chose a Samaritan, rather than a religious leader or lay associate, with whom the story's victim would have shared his land, as an example of love and neighbourliness. Neighbourliness, he indicates, should not be a function of geographical, cultural or ethnic proximity but a state of mind that transcends all these.

Yet it is still *neighbourliness* that is used as the metaphor for this mindset. The ideal of rootedness is not abandoned but, on the contrary, used to exemplify the standard of behaviour God requires from all. Irrespective of where the story's characters or audience came from, neighbourliness should be their proper goal and aspiration. And you are unlikely to be a neighbour to 'Samaritans' if you are not a neighbour to your neighbours.

From transport to mobility

These principles – of being rooted, having a stake in the community, respecting a sense of place, resisting insularity and protectionism, and recognizing one's own impermanence and accountability before God – call us to stand back from the immediate transport debate on fuel prices or rail infrastructure and engage with the broader issue of mobility by scrutinizing the unspoken assumptions that underlie much transport policy.

This is already being done in some quarters. The emergence of the environmental movement, growing calls for sustainable development and the goal of an integrated transport network all, in their own ways, challenge our basic assumption that we have a right to travel where we like, when we like and how we like. The biblical emphasis on rootedness, albeit in tension with mobility, encourages us to join in the same battle.

Hence, the first and most fundamental issue to consider is the all but unthinkable question: why should we be encouraging more mobility? It is a question that is, in fact, periodically asked, usually in response to specific plans for road expansion or a new airport terminal. But a periodic and location-specific debate is not enough. Rather than become 'nimbys' who critique mobility only when it impinges on our immediate circumstances, we need to articulate a coherent set of priorities and think through our society's hypermobility in a sustained and consistent way.

The traditional defence of mobility – that it facilitates economic growth – is technically correct but nowadays less than persuasive in the light of mounting evidence that economic growth and personal happiness become decoupled after a certain point (see Chapter 9). If more money does not make us happier, mobility loses its imperative. Indeed, the relational dislocation that hypermobility fosters actually makes us less happy. We are pursuing a mobility agenda to our own cost.

Addressing this question is not to preach a return to a pre-mobile society. The principles outlined above positively encourage mobility in so far as it builds healthy and just relationships and acts as an antidote to jealous, exclusive insularity. But they also require us to recognize and make some real choices, against which transport policies may be evaluated.

What is the environmental cost of our hypermobility and how does transport policy affect it? Is policy shaped by a desire to mollify the motorist, to boost air travel or to safeguard the environment – or does manifesto rhetoric pretend we can have it all? Do road-widening and airport-expansion plans have priority over local concerns, and should such conflicts be resolved by Whitehall or by local government? Circumstantial details will invariably affect particular decisions but political rhetoric that implies we can maintain hypermobility *and* environmental sustainability is misleading and dangerous.

In a similar way, what are the social costs of our hypermobility and how is transport policy affecting them? Are we sufficiently dedicated to neighbourhood cohesion to invest in public transport and restrict car use, as London has in recent years, in order to achieve it? Do we wish to see local transport infrastructure planned for the benefit of motorists, pedestrians or cyclists, for small local retailers or cheaper, out-of-town supermarkets?[23] Should local government have the final say in such matters or does central government have a role in restricting possible 'nimbyism'? Such questions are difficult, but they press upon us both the need to articulate priorities and the opportunity to develop a vision for local communities.

A Christian perspective rejects the simple dichotomy between the freedom and opportunity afforded by mobility and the constrictive obligations and duties imposed by rootedness. It is not either–or. Both have a role to play in shaping a relational society, but in doing so both must be seen as means rather than ends, to be used sparingly and even self-sacrificially in pursuit of the overall vision.

Ultimately, transport policy cannot *create* a relational, community-rich society, any more than health policy can guarantee a healthy one (see Chapter 7). If we are prepared to travel long distances to buy the cheapest products or to secure the next career move, the environmental and social costs of our hypermobility will simply grow. The situation is unlikely to improve until we recognize, both individually and collectively, the value of staying put.

Further engaging

Publications

Walter Brueggemann, *The Land: Place as Gift, Promise, and Challenge in Biblical Faith* (London: SPCK, 1978)

Michael Schluter, *Roots: Biblical Norm or Cultural Anachronism?* (Cambridge Papers, Vol. 4, No. 4, 1995)

Nick Spencer, *Where Do We Go from Here? A Biblical Perspective on Roots and Mobility in Britain Today* (Cambridge: Jubilee Centre, 2002)

Websites

John Adams, *The Social Implications of Hypermobility*: <http://www.geog.ucl.ac.uk/~jadams/publish.htm>

Department for Transport: <www.dft.gov.uk>

Office of the Deputy Prime Minister: <www.odpm.gov.uk>

Transport for London: <www.transportforlondon.gov.uk/tfl/>

❼ Health and Healthcare

Nigel Lawson once called the NHS 'the closest thing the English have to a religion'.[1] It is not hard to see what he meant.

The NHS has been one of the two or three most important issues facing the UK in the public mind for each of the last 15 years. Except for a handful of months when September 11th, the Iraq war and the fear of terrorism nudged ahead, it was deemed the most important issue in every month of Labour's second term. Health has been the public's top spending priority since records began in 1983.[2] It has been the prime candidate for extra public spending since then, and the most (for many people the *only*) justifiable reason for increasing taxation.[3] It even led to the election of the only independent MP in 2001, Dr Richard Taylor, a retired consultant, whose pledge to save Kidderminster Hospital won him the Wyre Forest seat. Healthcare is not the only public service and hospitals are not the only source of healthcare – the provision of mental-health services or care for the elderly at home is less visible but no less vital for the well-being of vulnerable members of society – yet that did not stop one hospital deciding the fate of a constituency. Health is so central to our well-being and the NHS so central to our experience of healthcare that, behind the economy, it has become *the* key election issue.

So pronounced is public concern for the NHS that it prompted Labour's biggest change of direction, in the 2002 Budget. Having followed the previous government's restrictive spending plans for five years, Gordon Brown announced a 1 per cent increase in employers' and employees' National Insurance contributions in order to provide 'a significant increase in resources for the NHS'.[4] The tax rise would finance a 7.4 per cent a year increase in NHS

This chapter focuses on issues of medical rather than social healthcare owing to a lack of space.

spending between 2002–3 and 2007–8 and push up the annual NHS budget to around £100 billion. Gordon Brown and Labour were prepared to risk 'back to tax and spend' headlines on the strength of public feeling about the NHS.

It was also a gamble in that research has shown that there has been no link between healthcare improvements and public opinion over the last 20 years. Since 1983, NHS spending has doubled in real terms, during which time the number of medical and dental staff has risen by 70 per cent, GP consultations by 13 per cent, outpatients by 20 per cent, accident and emergency patients by 30 per cent, and inpatients and day cases by 80 per cent, while the average waiting time for inpatients has fallen from ten to four months.[5] Over the same period, people's opinions and perceptions of the NHS have not only not improved but have actually worsened, with the net satisfaction level (i.e. the percentage of people satisfied minus those not satisfied) falling from 20 to −1. As one analyst of this trend has wryly noted, 'any of the nine different Secretaries of State for Health since 1983 would surely sigh in exasperation at an apparently ungrateful public'.[6]

Gordon Brown's spending pledge did, at least, establish the consensus that not only should the NHS be comprehensive, free at the point of delivery and available on the basis of need, but that it needed considerably higher investment to maintain these objectives. The real questions and the current political battle lines over the NHS and, to an extent all public services, thus became *how* it should be funded and *who* should provide the services.

The present central tax-funded system is not in immediate doubt, although some have floated the idea of an insurance-based system as exists in America, and new foundation trusts have the capacity to raise money themselves. There is more debate over who should *control* funding, with two of the key factors in the government's public-service modernization programme, devolution and flexibility,[7] encouraging greater financial autonomy for Primary Care Trusts and (in England) foundation hospitals, which, critics claim, will lead to a two-tier health system.

In terms of *who* should provide the services, there is general consensus over the need to dismantle the original NHS monopoly in favour of a mix of service provision from the state, private and voluntary sectors. The debate is over how the private sector should be used – whether directly by NHS patients or bought in via NHS managers – and how overall quality should be maintained, with Labour favouring centrally set targets regulated by an independent healthcare inspectorate, and the Conservatives rejecting all such centrally imposed standards in favour of hospitals setting their own targets which would then be regulated by market forces.

Underpinning both of these areas is the issue of choice, a buzzword for both major parties. Beneath the political consensus that 'consumers of public services should [. . .] be given the kind of options that they take for granted in other walks of life',[8] lie questions over whether patients should be able to choose between any hospital or a limited number, and whether they should choose directly or via a healthcare professional such as their GP. To what extent do we *want* a degree of paternalism in our health-service provision?

The dynamics of choice, however, are invariably shaped by the cultural context and, in particular, by the nature of the relationship between 'consumer' and health-service provider. If the context is one of aggressive, individualistic consumerism, choice can undermine a system in a way that it does not if the context is one of commitment, local ownership and mutual responsibility. Ultimately, the health of the nation and its health service has as much to do with their relationship to each other as with the size of any spending increase.

The concept of *shalom*

Turning to biblical teaching for guidance on modern, nationalized healthcare systems needs specific explanation. Any such system would have been unknown in the ancient Near East, with its ignorance of biomedicine and its pre-industrial culture. Primitive health practices do appear to be at the root of some of the Levitical laws,[9] but these, it has been argued, were 'primarily ceremonial and only at times of practical use in the prevention of disease'.[10]

Health and national healthcare systems are not just biomedical issues, however. The late Roy Porter's magisterial history of medicine, *The Greatest Benefit to Mankind*, has, broadly speaking, two intertwining plots.[11] The first is the story of medical discovery, of anatomy, dissection and bacteriology, and the second is the story of how such discoveries were used within society, the story of hospitals, slum clearances and vaccination programmes. As Ian McColl, former Professor of Surgery at Guy's and St Thomas' in London, has written:

It often comes as a surprise for some medical students that the health of a nation is more dependent on public health and social issues than the clinical activities of doctors. The reduction in tuberculosis over this [i.e. the twentieth] century in this country has much more to do with nutrition and housing than medicines.[12]

It is this aspect of healthcare – the ideological, attitudinal and social framework within which biomedicine takes place – about which biblical teaching offers guidance.

The ideological framework on which any healthcare system is built is the concept of health. A reductionist understanding of health naturally leads to the medicalization of life and an excessive demand on the healthcare provider. If my problems are in fact my body's problems, the solution lies not in my hands but in my doctor's. While there can be no questioning the organic reality of disease, a narrowly biomedical approach can miss the wood for the trees, analysing (and spending considerable sums of money treating) effects (such as liver cirrhosis) rather than causes (such as alcohol abuse resulting from loneliness or depression).

The biblical understanding of health, seen in the concept of *shalom* in the Old Testament and in the life and work of Christ in the New, is rather different.[13] Often simply translated 'peace', *shalom* is a 'holistic' term, incorporating physical, mental, emotional, relational and spiritual wholeness and, when used of a community, societal harmony. Different authorities define it as 'wholeness, well-being, vigour and vitality in all dimensions of human life' or 'pleasure and happiness, peace and well-being [. . .] overtones of justice [. . .] to live appropriately and to have harmony and balance in every aspect of one's life and relationships'.[14]

The difference in definitions is important as a holistic, relational and integrated concept of health not only encourages the involvement of the patient and the treatment of the person rather than the 'wound',[15] but also advises that the root causes of some physical ailments are in fact social, psychological or relational.

Directly linked to this is the question of responsibility and the attitudinal framework in which health systems operate. One of the principles behind the Torah was to represent Israel as a paradigm of love and care which would appeal to and attract other nations,[16] a principle that was also central to the spread of the early Church. The fraternal metaphor used repeatedly to describe Israel and the nascent Church is only one indication of the strength of the bond between people and, hence, of the responsibility they (should have) had for one other.[17]

This vision of siblings 'bear[ing] one another's burdens',[18] which is so fundamental to the idea of national healthcare provision, was not a substitute for personal responsibility, however. The autonomy and free will that are key to the biblical vision of humanity demand that each person is accountable. Living in an intricate web of load-bearing relationships does not exempt one from self-responsibility. Other people cannot be responsible for my health if I choose not to be.

This balance between mutual and self-responsibility also shapes the social framework of healthcare provision. The popular consumerist model of purchaser, provider, financial transaction, and product guarantee is, at best, of limited use for healthcare provision.

True health is difficult to recognize, difficult to realize and impossible to guarantee. It involves not simply a one-off transaction but instead the 'consumer's' long-term, full-time commitment just as much as it does the 'provider's' efficient and professional use of resources. You can't buy health.

The primary biblical model for relationships was covenantal rather than consumerist. The covenant was, in Jonathan Sacks' words, the Bible's answer 'to the most fundamental question in the evolution of societies: How can we establish relationships secure enough to become the basis of co-operation, without the use of economic, political or military power?'[19] It linked two parties in a relationship of on-going, mutual obligation and trust, through a voluntary oath of partnership:

> Covenant occurs when two individuals or groups [. . .] each acknowledging the integrity and sovereignty of the other, pledge themselves in mutual loyalty to achieve together what neither can achieve alone. Covenant is the use of language to create a bond of trust through the word given, the word received, the word honoured in mutual fidelity.[20]

There is, of course, no direct, biblical command that covenantal agreements should form the model for all relationships at all times and in all places, let alone those between citizen and healthcare provider several millennia later. Yet the centrality of covenant to the biblical narrative does at least point in this direction, and the fact that the quasi-healthcare role performed by the priests and the community's 'duty of care' to its most vulnerable members were both part of the great covenant ratified at the end of Deuteronomy also suggest that covenant is a more fruitful model than consumerism for aspects of public policy today.

Two final, if familiar, points of Christian teaching also bear repeating. The first is the persistent emphasis on caring for the weakest members of society. The orphan, widow and alien, those who were without a natural support network, were of particular interest to the law and the prophets, just as the vulnerable and the outcast were to Christ. In our understandable quest for efficiency, we must be careful not to treat those who demand greater attention and care as if they were 'bed-blockers'.

The second is that, in spite of, or perhaps because of, its well-drawn vision of *shalom*, biblical teaching is clear that, at least for the time being, full health is an unrealizable goal. We may strive for our *shalom* and that of our neighbour, community and society, but an awareness of sin counsels us against unrealistic expectations.

The responsibility of health

The manner in which these frameworks should shape our engagement with healthcare will be contentious and there is no reason to think that Christians will reach a consensus on the key questions of funding, service provision, regulation and choice. Technical and specific details, and extenuating and unforeseen circumstances, will make any absolute decision on these issues problematic.

The biblical emphases on *shalom*, self-responsibility and covenant do point in certain directions, however. During its second term, the Labour government had discussions about whether NHS treatment should be denied to obese people who refuse to lose weight. In the same way there is periodically a debate about the on-going treatment of smokers who ignore warnings to quit. For some any such policies constitute unacceptable state intervention into individuals' lives. For others they are a necessary measure if we wish to maintain a free-at-delivery, nationalized healthcare system.

The Christian vision rejects the idea that the state should run individuals' lives but also that individuals should ruin their own. Its concept of health and of covenant encourages policies in which individuals' self-responsibility lessens but does not abolish the burden of mutual responsibility.

This can take many forms. Public health education can encourage people to ignore drugs,[21] give up smoking, exercise regularly,[22] eat more healthily,[23] drink more sensibly,[24] and even (shock horror!) practise sexual abstinence and fidelity.[25] Public initiatives could extend the scheme of free provision of fruit to schoolchildren or reintroduce the free provision of milk at playtime. More punitively, government could regulate food-advertising claims stringently, place health warnings on certain foods or impose a tax on junk food. At its extreme, government could demand an agreement between healthcare provider and 'consumer' that required the latter to follow the former's advice in order to qualify for on-going treatment (although this would be hard to enforce and not a little controversial).

Many such initiatives – initiatives that recognize *shalom* by effectively extending healthcare from hospitals to homes – already exist and several major reports published during Labour's second term in office highlighted the need for prevention rather than cure.[26] One of these, the 2004 Wanless report, also underlined the importance of relationships in its recommendations, by advising 'the NHS [to] do more to improve the mental and physical well-being of its workforce'.[27]

This emphasis on relationships is important. The new, pluralistic and consumer-driven shape of the NHS has rapidly increased the number of working relationships healthcare professionals have, and placed an emphasis on collaboration within and between professions, and with organizational partners, policy makers, public representatives and patients.[28] The successful and efficient operation of the health service depends on the nature of these relationships. In the same way, dysfunctional, stressful or ineffective relationships often contribute to patients' ill-health, and measures intended to alleviate the stress on couples, families and employees have a direct if invisible impact on the healthcare system.[29]

Overall, the guidance for a Christian engagement with the issue of health and healthcare today tends towards the counter-cultural. This is partly in counselling against the unrealistic expectations that have done so much to decouple the NHS's real achievements over the last two decades from the public's perception of them.

Public-service devolution and the emphasis on choice have made politicians less accountable for the health service. If we want to pursue such modernization (and few wish to return to the paternalism of previous decades), we need to recognize that politicians have the power of football coaches rather than CEOs when dealing with the NHS.

It is also counter-cultural in its resistance to the medicalization of life, an attitude brilliantly captured in Malcolm Muggeridge's aphorism, 'I will lift up mine eyes unto the pills.' A Christian perspective sees health in holistic terms, not the holism of new-age 'healing' but (closer to) that of the World Health Organization's 'state of complete physical, mental and social well-being'.[30] Engaging with health and healthcare today will involve not simply ensuring that the National Health Service is well funded, but that it is relationally healthy itself, and that it works in partnership with, rather than instead of, patients and their representatives.

Further engaging

Publications

Andrew Fergusson (ed.), *Health: The Strength to be Human* (Leicester: IVP, 1993)

Roy Porter, *The Greatest Benefit to Mankind* (London: Fontana, 1997)

Nick Spencer, *Health and the Nation: A Biblical Perspective on Health and Healthcare in Britain Today* (Cambridge: Jubilee Centre, 2002)

Nicholas Timmins, *The Five Giants: A Biography of the Welfare State* (London: HarperCollins, 1995)

Charles Webster, *The National Health Service* (Oxford, Oxford University Press, 1998)

Websites

Christian Medical Fellowship: <www.cmf.org.uk>

Christian Nurses and Midwives: <www.cnm.org.uk>

❽ Criminal Justice

'Tough on crime, tough on the causes of crime' was Tony Blair's most inspired soundbite. In one instantly recognizable, advertising-literate catchphrase, Labour became the party of law and order without losing its reputation as the party of compassion and social justice.

The idea ran central to both 1997 and 2001 election manifestos:

> We believe in personal responsibility and in punishing crime, but also tackling its underlying causes [. . .] Government can help families and communities prevent crime. But when people do commit crimes, we need an effective criminal justice system able to catch, punish and rehabilitate people.[1]

According to the British Crime Survey (BCS), it is an approach that has met with some success.[2]

Overall crime levels have been falling since 1995, with the total number of crimes committed (as calculated by the British Crime Survey) falling from 16.5 million in 1997 to 12.3 million in 2002–3.[3] Since Labour first came to power in 1997, the overall level of burglary has fallen by 39 per cent, vehicle theft by 31 per cent and violent crime by 24 per cent.[4]

Despite this, public perception is that crime levels have increased over recent years. According to MORI's monthly polls, between a quarter and a third of the population consistently rate crime as one of the most important issues facing Britain today. Thirty-eight per cent of people believe that crime increased 'a lot' between 2001 and 2003, and 31 per cent in the previous two years.[5]

The reasons for this are varied. Media hype accounts for something (43 per cent of tabloid readers thought that the national crime rate had increased 'a lot' in 2001–3, compared with 26 per cent of broadsheet readers), as does the difference between local and national perception (people are more optimistic about crime levels in their own area than nationally).[6] The public also has an immutable belief in a golden age, in which life was safe and crimes were not committed.

Public concern is not entirely misplaced, however. Levels of violent crime have remained constant over recent years and the overall level of *recorded* crime[7] has increased since 1997. The crime detection rate stands at around 24 per cent and has fallen since 1980, failing to keep pace with the rise in recorded crime over this period.[8]

A longer-term perspective also reminds us that the recent fall in BCS crime levels merely returns the nation to the crime levels of the 1980s. *Recorded* crime levels (the only ones which offer long-term comparison) show that there are roughly ten times as many offences recorded per head of population today as there were 50 years ago (and twenty times as many violent offences) – and that is despite 50,000 more police officers and a three-fold rise in the prison population.[9] The 'golden age' may be a myth, but it is easy to see why the public believes the UK is a more hazardous and violent place today than half a century ago.

The reason for this long-term increase is, of course, a matter for debate. The brilliance of Tony Blair's soundbite was the way it synthesized and reconciled the two traditional explanations for crime: the 'left's' that it was the result of social injustice and the 'right's' that it was the result of personal immorality. Vice, Blair implied, was both learned *and* chosen, and demands a range of responses.

The fall in crime figures since 1997 suggests he is right, and that crime does demand a 'toolbox' approach. Recognizing this, and the fact that the range of possible responses is truly vast – from re-introducing the death penalty[10] to 'mak[ing] fewer things illegal',[11] – complicates rather than simplifies the problem, however. If a wide range of options is justifiably open to us, how should we decide which we favour? Should we be guided by the spirit of pragmatism and do what works (in so far as it is possible to tell) or are there ideological guidelines for our engagement with criminal justice?

The fact that crime is so intimately related to other major social issues should counsel us against pure pragmatism. Its link with social exclusion connects criminal justice to economics, as does its link with an affluent, possession-obsessed culture. The link to drug and alcohol abuse connects it to health and education policy. The link to hypermobility, rootlessness and social capital connects it to transport policy and to issues of asylum, immigration and community cohesion. Crime demands joined-up thinking, and policy initiatives driven solely by British Crime Survey statistics can miss the wood for the trees. Crime levels would no doubt fall if police and prisoner levels were doubled, but such a policy would not only be hugely expensive but would, to some extent, be treating the effect rather than the cause of criminality.

Instead, criminal justice demands a more principled engagement, which takes its place within a broader vision for society.

Righteousness and judgement

The idea and execution of justice is central to the biblical narrative. Justice is a fundamental characteristic and concern of God. 'I am the LORD, who exercises kindness, justice and righteousness on earth, for in these I delight.'[12] Justice has its roots in God's being, and as such is not only imperative, but personal and relational rather than abstract and propositional.

This is seen in the two words commonly used for 'justice' in the Old Testament. The first of these, *tsedeq(ah)*, usually translated 'righteous(ness)', comes from a root meaning 'straight' and refers to being in accordance with the norms revealed and embodied by God, norms that are relational:

Tsdq [. . .] refers to a relationship between two parties and implies behaviour which fulfils the claims arising from such an involvement. *Tsdq* [. . .] is the fulfilment of the demands of a relationship, with God or a person. There is no norm of righteousness outside of that personal involvement. When people fulfil the conditions imposed on them by relationships, they are righteous.[13]

The second word, *mishpat*, usually translated 'judge', refers to 'what needs to be done if people and circumstances are to be restored to conformity with *tsedeq* [. . .] to uphold and restore right relationships'.[14] This entailed adjudication *and* punishment in such a way as would restore and renew the moral order, and had a positive rather than negative objective. *Mishpat* was about liberating the oppressed and promoting the equity and harmony of the community rather than just overthrowing oppressors and disciplining evildoers.

These interlinked concepts are seen in the two biblical archetypes of justice, the exodus and the cross. The object of the exodus is not to punish the Egyptians or even to free the slaves, although both these are achieved. Rather, as Moses and Aaron tell Pharaoh, God's command is to 'let my people go *so that they may hold a festival to me in the desert*', one of the reasons why the book of Exodus ends with the presence of God coming to dwell with his people.[15] Similarly, the cross enacts the defeat of sin and the liberation of creation, not just for the sake of liberation but so that all creation may be restored into right relationship with the creator, and humanity drawn to him as a renewed family.[16]

These concerns mark the criminal legislation in the Torah. Superficial readings of this cite the *lex talionis*, 'an eye for an eye', as the basis of and justification for an entirely retributive system of criminal justice, without realizing that the law is specific to its narrative context of personal injuries, and intended as a means of guiding compensation levels and as an antidote to the blood-feud principle that would otherwise result in escalating vengeance.[17]

Instead, the *lex talionis* advocates the *principle* of retributive justice as against that of a purely utilitarian approach. This latter understands that 'punishment is justified only if it can be proven to benefit society by reducing future crime', and sentences the offender accordingly. However, this also means that the criminal 'is not treated as an autonomous person who is accountable for his moral choices but as a manipulable variable in a social equation [. . .] simply as a means to an end'.[18] The *lex talionis* insists that individuals should be treated as independent, moral beings, responsible for their actions and accountable for their crimes.

The law does allow for a deterrent element, as indicated in the repeated formula, 'all Israel will hear [of this punishment] and be afraid, and no-one among you will do such an evil thing again', and this point is borne out in the educative and communal thinking that runs through the Torah's criminal legislation.[19] Justice is of vital importance to the existence and flourishing of Israel itself. 'Follow justice and justice alone, so that you may live and possess the land the LORD your God is giving you', the people are told in Deuteronomy.[20] 'Cursed is the man who withholds justice from the alien, the fatherless or the widow', they hear later on.[21] It was important to be impartial,[22] trustworthy[23] and subject to due process.[24]

Perhaps most significantly, it was to be a community activity. Crime was seen not so much as the contravention of state laws as a breakdown in the relationship between offender and victim or between offender and community. Thus, the criminal justice system was decentralized, with 'judges and officials [appointed] for each of your tribes in every town'.[25] The law was not written in 'legalese' but addressed to all the people[26] and subsequently given wide publicity.[27] Witnesses were required to volunteer themselves at a hearing and were blameworthy if they chose to keep silent.[28] Capital punishment was administered only on the basis of multiple witnesses and then by the community as a whole.[29] Corporal punishment was to be administered in the presence of the judges who condemned the guilty, and was limited so that 'your brother will [not] be degraded in your eyes'.[30] At every step along the way the community was implicated and educated, as the law communicated social norms and inculcated moral values.

Much legislation was directly about relational restitution between victim and offender. Some laws, particularly those pertaining to theft and personal injury, required the offender to pay the victim a disproportionate figure, which had the effect of acting as a disincentive as well as 'forcing the offender to stand in the victim's shoes, suffering a loss equal to the victim's loss at their hands'.[31] Others imposed a duty on the perpetrator of a physical assault to see that his victim was 'completely healed' and to 'pay the injured man for the loss of his time'.[32]

This retributive, symbolic, educative and relational function of the law is mirrored in the New Testament, not so much in the few, short references to 'authorities', which are to be respected for being 'sent by [God] to punish those who do wrong and to commend those who do right', but in the passages on church discipline.[33] This was profoundly relational and could therefore be especially painful. 'Brothers' were to 'carry each other's burdens' and the strong were to be careful not to exercise their freedom in such a way as to 'become a stumbling-block to the weak'.[34] Yet, immorality was not to be tolerated, with Christ advising conflicts to be settled at first by discussion 'just between the two of you', then in the presence of 'one or two others [. . .] so that "every matter may be established by the testimony of two or three witnesses"', and then before the whole church'.[35]

The last resort of expelling the immoral brother from the community, was, as Paul makes clear, a deliberate echo of similar commands in Deuteronomy.[36] But even then, as Paul writes, when 'the punishment inflicted on [the wrongdoer] by the majority is sufficient for him', the church is 'to forgive and comfort him [. . . and] reaffirm your love for him'.[37] In a similar vein, when Paul writes to Timothy, he advises him to rebuke 'publicly [those who sin] so that the others may take warning',[38] and to the Thessalonians that 'If anyone does not obey our instruction in this letter [. . .] Do not associate with him, in order that he may feel ashamed. Yet do not regard him as an enemy, but warn him as a brother.'[39]

In these microcosms of local church discipline we see the legal principles of the Torah embodied. Because 'crime' is a breakdown of relationship, it is best addressed by relational measures. These could involve financial reparation, 'reintegrative shaming' or, in extreme cases, the social alienation of church expulsion or the Israelite cities of refuge.[40] They could have a deliberate, socially educative intent, while maintaining a retributive principle at heart. But their ultimate objective was the reaffirmation of the *tsedeqah* that was so central to God's being and his creation.

Justice and the community[*]

These key Christian insights, that crime is an issue of relational breakdown rather than legislative contravention and that justice is a process of re-establishing the social order by means of restoring the moral order, have several significant implications.

First, they shift the emphasis from a discussion of the 'causes of crime' to one of the *tsedeqah* of the community. 'Crime control and criminal justice have come to be disconnected from the broader themes of social justice and social reconstruction',[41] and there is a real need to reconnect them. This has been addressed in part by the establishment of the Social Exclusion Unit,[42] but there remains a need to promote a positive vision for society, what Israel understood from the term *tsedeqah* (and *shalom*) and what Oliver Letwin, in a 2001 speech, called 'the neighbourly society':

> It is the formation of character within the family and within the wider community that can alone lead us from broken communities and broken laws towards the neighbourly society. To deprive a child of the support and kindly discipline that forms character is to commit an act of inhumanity, to start the child on the conveyor belt to a life of crime. The object of policy must be to bolster those institutions that can provide the character-formation which is the indispensable precondition of neighbourliness. A great part of the burden has to be borne by our schools and teachers.[43]

* This section draws heavily on Jonathan Burnside's chapter on criminal justice in *Jubilee Manifesto*.

This inevitably links criminal justice policy to other areas, a further reason for joined-up, ideologically motivated social thinking. It also calls for a shift in political rhetoric, from individual rights to community responsibilities,[44] and from tough anti-crime legislation towards an articulation of positive community living or 'neighbourliness'. It should be emphasized that this is not to advocate an especially lenient or purely utilitarian approach to criminal justice, as the foundational principle of retributive justice remains important in the overall objective of restoring the moral and social order. Nor is it to remove the need for widespread, effective and visible policing, a promise of most political manifestos.

Second, the relational vision calls for a greater emphasis on the role of the victim. This is not the same as a media-generated 'collective moral outrage' in which 'victims serve a useful function in a pluralistic moral order [because] we do not agree on right and wrong'.[45] Instead, it means ensuring that the criminal justice process takes sufficient account of the needs and interests of victims of crime, such as by giving greater scope for contact or negotiations between victims and offenders (where this is desirable) or ensuring a greater role for imaginative forms of reparation and restitution.

Third, it means rethinking prison. Biblical teaching does allow for some form of social-exclusion punishment, but the manner and extent to which it is used today is unhelpful.[46] The prison population of England and Wales has risen from 49,000 ten years ago to 75,000 today. England and Wales have the highest imprisonment rate in the European Union at 141 per 100,000 of the population. The 15,200 additional prison places provided since 1995 have cost an estimated £2 billion. Fifty-nine per cent of prisoners are reconvicted within two years of being released, and this rises to 74 per cent for men under 21. The Social Exclusion Unit has calculated that re-offending by ex-prisoners costs society at least £11 billion per year. Seventy-seven per cent of prisoners who had used drugs before their sentence admit to taking them after their release.

Around a third of all prisoners released in England and Wales have nowhere to live on release, despite the fact that stable accommodation can reduce re-offending by over 20 per cent.

Perhaps most significantly from a relational point of view, 45 per cent of offenders lose contact with their families during their sentence, in spite of the fact that, as Home Office research shows, 'good family ties can reduce a prisoner's risk of re-offending by six times'. In September 2003, over 25,000 prisoners were held over 50 miles from their committal-court town and 10,880 were held over 100 miles away. Perhaps not surprisingly, the number of prison visits has fallen by a third over the past five years, despite a rise of more than 20 per cent in the prison population.

This woeful list is no reason to abandon incarceration altogether, but rather to rethink its objective, in the light of its evident failings and enormous financial and social cost. Rather than generating a state of 'arrested development', punishment 'should assist in this process of maturation and personal development [. . .] and [. . .] foster "generativity" (that is, benefit to others), [such as through] mutual help societies, volunteering, community service, restitution projects and active engagement in parenting'.[47] Prison regimes themselves could encourage projects such as the Kairos Community, a Christian rehabilitation programme, which, according to a Board of Visitors report into Verne prison in Dorset, 'is one of the most successful programmes contributing to rehabilitation and continues to be a steadying and civilising influence'.[48]

Finally, and linked to this point, there is a need to establish the communal nature of the problem, and for the state to involve and draw on the strengths of local communities, rather than trying to 'solve' it by removing undesirables from society and placing them in 'invisible institutions'. This would involve fostering the local accessibility and accountability of the criminal justice process, in courts, affiliated services and local prisons. It would also mean informing local communities about criminal justice and cultivating a sense of local ownership of prisons as there is with schools and hospitals.[49]

Ultimately, how we deal with crime says a great deal about how we understand ourselves. The danger, in a culture marked by materialism and individualism, is that retribution is considered sufficient and criminals are amputated from society so that it may be healed. Yet, if we profess a biblical view of humanity, so neatly encapsulated in the Ubuntu proverb, 'a person is a person through other persons', we will acknowledge the communal tragedy of crime and seek a communal response.

Further engaging

Publications

Jonathan Burnside, *Licence to Kill?* (Cambridge Papers, Vol. 11, No. 2, June 2002)

Jonathan Burnside and Nicola Baker (eds), *Relational Justice: Repairing the Breach* (Winchester: Waterside Press, 1994, reprinted 2004)

Jonathan Burnside *et al.*, *Religion & Rehabilitation: Faith-Based Therapeutic Communities in Prison* (Cullompton: Willan Publishing, forthcoming)

Julian Rivers, *Beyond Rights: The Morality of Rights-Language* (Cambridge Papers, Vol. 6, No. 3, September 1997)

Christopher Townsend, *An Eye for an Eye?: The Morality of Punishment* (Cambridge Papers, Vol. 6, No. 1, March 1997)

Paternoster Press's Christian Perspectives series includes books on law reform, human rights and legal philosophy, law and relationism, the limits of the law, and law and justice.

Websites

Churches' Criminal Justice Forum: <www.ccjf.org>

Kairos Prison Ministry: <www.kairosprisonministry.org.uk>

Lawyers' Christian Fellowship: <www.lawcf.org>

Prison Reform Trust: <www.prisonreformtrust.org.uk>

Relational Justice Bulletin: <www.relationshipsfoundation.org>

❾ The Economy

Economies decide elections. We wish it were not so and we often pretend it isn't. In 1992 the British public convinced everyone, including itself, that it was more motivated by Labour's focus on public services than by the Conservatives' promise to cut taxes. The shock election result revealed the truth: people did not trust Labour with their money and this, ultimately, trumped all other concerns. This could be interpreted positively, as the prudent desire to enable long-term investment in public services, or negatively, as pure greed, but either way the message was clear: 'It's the economy, stupid!'

Labour's remarkable transformation in the mid-1990s hinged on convincing the electorate that the party was economically trustworthy. The party promised not to raise income tax and Gordon Brown tied its spending plans to the Conservatives' (although he did raise indirect taxes beyond previous levels). The strategy worked. Indeed, it worked so successfully that Labour's 2001 election posters focused on Tory economic incompetence in a way that would have been unthinkable a decade earlier.[1]

Commentators generally agree that the economy has been Labour's strongest hand throughout its second term. The party's record on economic growth and stability has been widely commended. The UK economy has grown in every quarter since the 2001 election. Unemployment fell to 4.8 per cent in 2004. Consumer Price Index (CPI) inflation[2] has remained below 1.5 per cent for over two years and has been among the lowest in the EU since 2000.

The government's record on redistribution and income equality has been more mixed. Over recent years Britain has experienced the 'unusual combination' of 'slightly rising income inequality and falling relative poverty'. The gap between the very rich and the rest has widened while many poorer families have seen their incomes rise faster than the average, a result that can be directly attributed to the government's tax-and-benefit policy.[3] In spite of this, Britain is still one of the most economically unequal countries in Europe, with around 14 per cent of the population and 19 per cent of children living in a household with an income less than half the national average.[4]

Behind the government's record on growth and equality, there are, however, some worrying signs. Economic growth has been made possible by an ever more pervasive culture of consumer debt, with money owed on cards, mortgages, loans and overdrafts now totalling £1 trillion, an unprecedented figure that may, in the Bank of England's words, pose 'considerable challenges' to UK financial stability. Running concurrent with this, a sense of an impending pensions crisis, due to an ageing population, a small basic state pension and a substantial pension-fund deficit among UK firms, is worrying government, disaffecting employees and forcing a major re-evaluation of the idea of retirement.[5]

Perhaps most worryingly, there are serious questions about the environmental and social sustainability of current economic growth levels. The vast increase in personal mobility (see Chapter 6), in road freight traffic, in air transport of people and goods; the huge demands placed on domestic and international food producers by the small number of excessively powerful food retailers; the pressure on land usage and social infrastructure exerted by the rising population level that a growing economy demands: each of these trends casts doubt on the sustained growth of the British economy and thereby on the prospects of income parity.

These trends also point towards a submerged but equally serious challenge facing modern Britain. Economic growth is no longer delivering what it was always declared it would: happiness. Nothing is more axiomatic to the modern mind than the idea that economic growth benefits society, an idea that is demonstrably true *up to a point*. Mounting evidence shows that above a certain level, income and happiness are decoupled.[6] Richer societies are not necessarily happier ones. Richer people are not necessarily more satisfied with life.

UK GDP per capita has risen by around 300 per cent in the

post-war period, as have disposable-income levels, and, accordingly, most Britons today live in a material paradise unimaginable in 1945.[7] Yet levels of happiness and life-satisfaction are no higher today than they were in the 1950s and in many comparable societies they are actually lower. Over the same period, levels of clinical depression, suicide, alcohol addiction and crime have risen considerably. In the words of one economist, 'people in the West [. . .] have become much richer, they work much less, they have longer holidays, they travel more, they live longer, and they are healthier. But they are no happier.'[8]

This will make instinctive sense to many people, and is confirmed by studies of human happiness that suggest that satisfaction with life is fostered by good, close relationships, social participation, a sense of self-esteem, control over one's life, a sense of meaning and purpose, serious religious commitment, physical comfort, and material wealth.[9] Our obsessive pursuit of the last of these in recent decades has secured the penultimate good and weakened all the others. When money becomes the measure of all things, those things that can't be priced aren't valued.[10]

Underlying, therefore, the important and, during election time, prominent issues of economic growth and equality, is the almost sacrilegious question of objectives: should we be pursuing growth in the way we have been over recent decades, and if not, what should be our goal and how might it be achieved?

What is money *for?*

In spite of popular belief to the contrary, biblical teaching does not simply reject money and advocate penury for all. Instead, it embraces it within a broader vision of loving God, serving one another and stewarding creation.

The repeated affirmation of creation's goodness in Genesis chapter 1 is the foundation stone for our understanding of money. Money is, in reality, simply an abstraction from creation, a language or tool by means of which we manipulate the world. Given creation's inherent if marred goodness, money cannot be evil in itself. Just as creation exists to be celebrated and enjoyed, so do money and that which it provides. 'When God gives any man wealth and possessions, and enables him to enjoy them, to accept his lot and be happy in his work – this is a gift of God.'[11]

The critical difference between this outlook and that of modern material consumerism is that in embracing the goodness of material wealth, the Christian vision embeds it firmly in a broader context. First, wealth is contingent on God. Much as we like to predict, plan for and secure the future through judicious investment, tomorrow will inevitably have problems of its own.[12] As David prays during the lavish consecration of the Temple in 1 Chronicles chapter 29:

Everything comes from you, and we have given you only what comes from your hand. We are aliens and strangers in your sight [. . .] Our days on earth are like a shadow [. . .] all this abundance that we have provided for building you a temple [. . .] comes from your hand, and all of it belongs to you.[13]

Second, wealth is dangerous. Its unique ability to become master rather than servant earns it a number of sharp 'handle with care' warnings. Christ's fearsome words that 'it is easier for a camel to go through the eye of a needle than for a rich man to enter the kingdom of God' are spoken, not because money is evil, but because he recognizes that 'where your treasure is, there your heart will be also', and because he has just witnessed a young man lose everything for the sake of his 'great wealth'.[14] Similarly, Paul's equally famous monetary aphorism is not, in fact, about money but about its dangers:

People who want to get rich fall into temptation and a trap and into many foolish and harmful desires that plunge men into ruin and destruction. For the love of money is a root of all kinds of evil. Some people, eager for money, have wandered from the faith and pierced themselves with many griefs.[15]

Third, monetary wealth entails certain responsibilities, namely to 'Love the Lord your God with all your heart and with all your soul and with all your mind [. . . and to] love your neighbour as yourself'.[16] Time and again the objective of making money for these reasons is seen in particular individuals and situations. The book of Proverbs lauds the 'wife of noble character' because she 'work[s] vigorously [and] her trading is profitable', *and* because she 'opens her arms to the poor and extends her hands to the needy'.[17] Christ commanded his followers to 'use worldly wealth to gain friends for yourselves, so that when it is gone, you will be welcomed into eternal dwellings'.[18] Paul wrote to the Ephesians advising that 'He who has been stealing must steal no longer, but must work, doing something useful with his own hands, that he may have something to share with those in need'.[19]

It is this vision – that wealth is good and to be enjoyed but contingent, dangerous and, above all, an instrument for building up relationships – that informs the economic system outlined in the Torah.[20] This details a market-based economy in which trading for profit was acceptable and indeed, encouraged, within certain limits. The role of the state, in the guise of the king, was restricted (quite remarkably so given the quasi-divine nature of the king in many ancient Near Eastern societies). The level of taxation was capped and proportional, and a well-defined legal code established property rights and made provision for debt collection. Universal property ownership was established and, through the Jubilee legislation, maintained. Restrictions were imposed on the labour market through the Sabbath and sabbatical-year regulations, rootedness was encouraged, interest on loans was prohibited, and, as far as it is possible to tell, a stable monetary system and price level ensued.

The result of this was a system that encouraged trade and competition but prevented excessive accumulation of economic power, and precluded the social and economic inequalities of a wholly unfettered market system. By placing restrictions on land, labour and capital the market was firmly embedded within a culture that placed relationships above returns and used wealth to build up people rather than people to build up wealth.

Relationships before riches

The complexity of many economic questions prevents most people from engaging with them in any detail. Election campaigns, for all their emphasis on the economy, tend not to provide opportunities for comprehensive scrutiny of macro-economic policy, or of the agenda of the anti-capitalism/globalization movement, which has been so prevalent over recent years. Accordingly, neither the specific implications of the economic system outlined in the Torah nor the anti-capitalism movement are discussed here, although both may be pursued via the 'Further engaging' section below.

Instead, the job of Christians who wish to evaluate economic policies at election time, without the benefit of economic expertise, is to critique the vision that motivates such policies and the rhetoric they inspire. One way of doing this is to ask the almost un-askable question: Why, if life-satisfaction becomes decoupled from wealth after a certain point, are we exhausting ourselves on a growth treadmill? If the vision that has inspired governments for decades, of societies becoming more contented as they become wealthier, is dissolving before our eyes, what do we have to replace it with?

This critique becomes more pointed when supplemented by the question of at what *cost* our economic growth comes, a question with implications for numerous areas of public policy. If the labour mobility that powers our economic growth is tearing up communities and fostering crime, is it worth it? If the long-hours culture that generates business efficiency and competitiveness is wrecking family and home life, is it worth it? Is economic growth a sufficient reason to demand mass immigration, particularly when those immigrants are invited to do the work that British-born people do not, apparently, wish to do themselves?[21] In each of these cases a Christian perspective that views wealth creation as a tool of society's relational health is likely to be at odds with current political orthodoxies.

These questions demand further lines of engagement, ones that directly address those factors that prioritize money over people, and that try to embed the market in a more relational context. One such line of engagement would involve tighter regulation of the UK's enormous debt culture.[22] When *average* personal debt in the UK, excluding mortgages, is £5,300; when personal debt has grown twice as fast as income since 1997; when Britons owe £54 billion on credit cards; when nearly a quarter of the population are worried they will not be able to maintain their debt repayments; when a quarter of those in debt are receiving treatment for stress, depression and anxiety from their family doctor; when money is a bigger cause of relationship rows than infidelity: when the nation's debt culture is this serious and causing this much personal grief without any obvious compensation in the level of people's life satisfaction, there is a real need to review credit laws.

This might involve tightening up the laws that govern the marketing of consumer credit; sharing information on debtors via a central register; clarifying and simplifying credit agreements; abolishing long-term credit ties; abolishing penalties for early debt repayment; scrutinizing debt management companies; confronting loan sharks and other irresponsible lenders; or expanding debt advice services. Many of these measures were outlined in the Department of Trade and Industry's 2003 White Paper on the consumer credit market, but to date, too little has been done to break up the relatively recent British love affair with debt.[23]

A second line of engagement would involve entrenching sustainable development principles and practice within government, private and public sectors at all levels. In a five-year review of the government's sustainability strategy, the Sustainable Development Commission outlined a series of 20 challenges to government, intended to stimulate further action in an area that has sometimes been overlooked in the pursuit of economic growth.[24] Sustainable development should be at the heart of national, regional and local government; play a central role in all aspects of the economy's management; be incorporated in key cross-departmental processes such as the Budget and the Comprehensive Spending Review; be embedded in the school education process; be explained more clearly to businesses and the public; and be made a requirement in business practice.

A third line would involve addressing the UK's culture of long working hours. Although this is rather more difficult to measure than is often assumed, particularly with the rise of part-time, remote and portfolio working, it is generally agreed that the British work the longest hours in Europe.[25] This, combined with increased participation in the workplace and longer commuting distances, has resulted in a rising domestic time deficit: put simply, people spend less time at home.

Not only is this culture of long working hours and its attendant domestic time deficit detrimental to people's non-work relationships, but there is evidence that it 'is having serious repercussions on their motivation at work'.[26] Addressing this will be controversial, but lessons can be learned from other European countries.[27] In France, the Aubry laws have been effective in reducing the number of people working over 35 hours a week; in Denmark, a 1987 agreement on working time has led to 45 per cent of all employees working fewer than 37 hours per week; in Sweden, the Working Hours Act sets a standard working week of 40 hours and has helped over half of all workers to work below 40 hours a week: none of these measures has led to an economic meltdown.[28] Ending the current, widely used UK opt-out on the European Working Time Directive may improve life satisfaction without having any cataclysmic effect on competitiveness.

Finally, and perhaps most importantly, strengthening non-monetary relationships is the most powerful way of subverting the principles of a society that has forgotten what economic growth is *for*. Such an objective might entail encouraging voluntary work and the voluntary sector, which, despite having expanded to 2 per cent of the total workforce, actually employs fewer volunteers than in the past.[29] It might involve exploring and popularizing different approaches to measuring social well-being and progress: the Human Development Index,[30] the Genuine Progress Indicator,[31] or the Measure of Domestic Progress,[32] instead of the traditional Gross Domestic Product. It might involve the development of new currencies, such as time, as a means of building relationships and 'social capital'.[33] Supremely, it would mean protecting and fostering family life, the biggest and most important residue of non-monetary relationships in any society, the health of which has an incalculable effect on the health, wealth and well-being of society at large.[34]

Managing the economy is, behind defence and security, the principle role of government. Ensuring growth, stability and a degree of wealth parity are its quite proper objectives, rightly scrutinized at election time. But economies are not pre-programmed vehicles that can be sped up, slowed down, and stabilized but not steered. In reality, they are embedded in and shaped by society and the aspirations of its citizens. Although no modern Western government, even one that controls as high a proportion of GDP as the current UK one, can autonomously steer its economy towards a predetermined destination, it can, at least, encourage such a change of direction. As we damage our environment and grow wealthier without getting any happier, we are in real need of just such a change of direction.

Further engaging

Publications

Clive Hamilton, *Growth Fetish* (London: Pluto Press, 2004: <www.growthfetish.com>)

Paul Mills, *The Ban on Interest: Dead Letter or Radical Solution?* (Cambridge Papers, Vol. 2, No. 1, March 1993)

Paul Mills, *Faith versus Prudence? Christians and Financial Security* (Cambridge Papers, Vol. 4, No. 1, March 1995)

Paul Mills, *Investing as a Christian: Reaping Where You Have Not*

Sown? (Cambridge Papers, Vol. 5, No. 2, June 1996)

Paul Mills, *The Divine Economy* (Cambridge Papers, Vol. 9, No. 4, December 2000)

Michael Schluter, *Risk, Reward and Responsibility: Limited Liability and Company Reform* (Cambridge Papers, Vol. 9, No. 2, June 2000)

Michael Schluter and David Lee, *The R Factor* (London: Hodder & Stoughton, 1993)

Nick Spencer, *The Measure of All Things? A Biblical Perspective on Money and Value in Britain Today* (Cambridge: Jubilee Centre, 2003)

Christopher Townsend, *Render unto Caesar? The Dilemmas of Taxation Policy* (Cambridge Papers, Vol. 10, No. 3, September 2001)

Websites

Richard Layard, *Happiness: Has Social Science a Clue?* (London School of Economics: Lionel Robins Memorial Lectures 2002/3 <http://cep.lse.ac.uk/events/lectures/layard/RL030303.pdf>).

Consumer Credit Counselling Service: <www.cccsintl.org>

Credit Action: <www.creditaction.org.uk>

JustShare: <www.justshare.org.uk>

Keep Time for Children: <www.keeptimeforchildren.org.uk>

Andrew Oswald (academic, with special interest in, among other things, happiness data): <www.andrewoswald.com>

Conclusion: Voting Wisely

This book will not have told readers whom to vote for. It will not have revealed what that mythical beast, the Christian Political Party, looks like. It will not even have outlined what a Christian election manifesto must say. Politics is too complex and protean an exercise to be susceptible to ideologically driven, definitive solutions.

This should not be read as a counsel of despair, however. The health of any democracy depends on its electorate's level of knowledge and involvement. A nation whose public understands or cares little about the issues over which elections are fought is prey to the soundbite and the image. Serious thought and engagement is the only truly effective antidote to political sloganeering and a culture of spin. If nothing else, this book hopes to have outlined some of the more pressing social and political issues of the day, so that readers may critique party manifestos and broadcasts more confidently and so that the democratic health of the nation may, in some small measure, be advanced.

It hopes, however, to have done more than that. 'The Christian policy' may be a dangerous, hubristic phrase but 'the non-Christian policy' is not. The relational vision at the heart of the Christian faith may not be able to prescribe exactly how Christians should respond to the single European currency or university top-up fees, but it can critique and even proscribe policies that, for example, alienate asylum applicants, treat immigrants as fuel for the economy, or regard criminals as problems rather than people.

More positively, a thoughtful Christian engagement with politics can offer a vision that will stabilize and guide thinking on the seemingly disparate social issues facing the UK today. A recurring theme throughout these chapters has been how political issues are inextricably intertwined. One cannot engage seriously with asylum without having thought through attitudes to immigration, citizenship and the international order, or with transport policy without some consideration of economy, environment and social cohesion.

A pragmatic approach to politics is essential when dealing with specific policy initiatives, whose effectiveness should ideally be tested before implementation. When that pragmatism moves from specific policies to the broader political vision, however, the result can be harmful, with government departments working not in partnership according to a shared vision, but independently according to specific, limited objectives, the very antithesis of the joined-up thinking that is so popular in current political rhetoric. Having an overarching political vision may not make solving social problems, let alone addressing political 'events', significantly easier. No voter should underestimate the relentless, distorting pressure of circumstance on modern government. Yet, a shared vision does at least have a coherent robustness that encourages intellectual cross-fertilization and policy efficiency.

Perhaps most importantly, this book hopes to have afforded a moment for *self*-reflection. As mentioned in the Introduction, elections should not simply be treated as occasions for the public to sit in judgement on its leaders, praising or abusing them for having met or failed its objectives. In a modern, liberal, free-market society, governments cannot govern *for* the people. As Tony Blair said in 2002:

> After five years in government I know only too well that passing legislation, or making a speech, will not solve vandalism on estates, raise standards in secondary schools, look after the elderly at risk. The job of government is to provide investment, support and infrastructure for those trying to solve problems at the local level.[1]

Sitting in judgement on elected politicians is entirely right and just, but doing so without a corresponding act of self-examination is hypocritical and ultimately fruitless. Elections provide just such an opportunity for self-examination and this book has, hopefully, helped readers to reflect on their own objectives for society, while encouraging them to view and adopt 'relational thinking' as the key Christian insight in shaping the social order.

Exactly how this process of self-reflection inclines readers to vote will vary. As mentioned in the Introduction, the issues covered in this book mirror domestic public concern as recorded by MORI and consequently only touch on several of the most pressing issues facing the world today. Some readers will view environmental degradation or global poverty as trumping all other issues discussed here and will vote accordingly.

Others will feel that their objectives are so easily lost in the detail and complexity of specific policy initiatives that politicians' perceived values and integrity provide the best guide to voting. This is a reasonable strategy providing that scrutiny of a politician's or a party's values and objectives is not a substitute for self-reflection. Voting for leaders because their objectives appear close to yours is wholly different from voting for them because they seem nice.

Still others will prioritize their social concerns, apply a Christian critique to them and then compare them with those articulated in party manifestos. Time-consuming as this process may be, it is perhaps the most robust and reliable way of casting one's vote, with the perceived difference between personal and party concerns acting as a spur to further engagement.

Whichever strategy one uses, a Christian approach that rejects the sacred–secular divide and accords significance to every aspect of human life will see voting as a form of worship. The fact that we in the UK live in a democracy, in which the actions of our leaders are taken in our name, further underlines its importance. Voting may not be easy if it demands a difficult prioritization of issues. It may not be particularly appealing if the options available fail to inspire allegiance. And it is certainly not the end of political participation. But it is an important right and responsibility for those who live in a democracy, and Christians owe it to God, to their neighbours and to themselves to vote wisely.

Notes

Introduction: Politics, Politicians and the Public Today

1 <www.electoralcommission.gov.uk/about-us/election01results.cfm>.
2 *Hansard*, Vol. 370, Part 5, Column 47, 20 June 2001.
3 <www.mori.com/polls/2001/elec_comm_rep.shtml>.
4 C. Bromley and J. Curtice, 'Where have all the voters gone?', in A. Park *et al.* (eds), *British Social Attitudes: The 19th Report* (Aldershot: Ashgate, 2002).
5 *None of the Above: Non-Voters and the 2001 Election* (Hansard Society, 2001; <www.mori.com/polls/2001/pdf/hansard2.pdf>).
6 <http://news.bbc.co.uk/1/hi/uk_politics/1845276.stm>.
7 J. Curtice and B. Seyd, 'Is there a crisis of political participation?', in A. Park *et al.* (eds), *British Social Attitudes: The 20th Report* (Aldershot: Ashgate, 2003).
8 It should be noted that the number of people who claim to have participated in non-electoral political activity is always higher than the number of people who actually have participated.
9 Curtice and Seyd, 'Is there a crisis of political participation?'
10 See <www.psr.keele.ac.uk/area/uk/man.htm> for all party manifestos since 1945.
11 See <www.mori.com/polls/trends/issues.shtml>.
12 Health, education and crime were all seen as more important than asylum, nationhood and the international order. The economy was not viewed as being as important an issue as any of these but, as the relevant chapters explain, this can be misleading. Transport was seen as the least important of the issues discussed here, but that, as the chapter argues, is because we fail to link it with the crucial question of mobility, which has much wider implications.

1 Political Ideas Today

1 J. Curtice and S. Fisher, 'The power to persuade? A tale of two Prime Ministers', in *British Social Attitudes: The 20th Report*.
2 A. Park and P. Surridge, 'Charting change in British values', in *British Social Attitudes: The 20th Report*.
3 T. Bentley and J. Wilsdon (eds), *The Adaptive State: Strategies for Personalising the Public Realm* (London: DEMOS, 2003).

4   See Derek Wanless, *Securing Good Health for the Whole Nation* (London: Stationery Office, 2004; <www.hm-treasury.gov.uk/consultations_and_legislation/wanless/consult_wanless04_final.cfm>).

5   See, for example, Richard Reeves, *The Politics of Happiness* (London: New Economics Foundation, 2003); Richard Layard, *Happiness: Has Social Science a Clue?* (London School of Economics: Lionel Robbins Memorial Lectures 2002/3); Clive Hamilton, *Growth Fetish* (London: Pluto Press, 2004); N. Donovan and D. Halpern, *Life Satisfaction: the State of Knowledge and Implications for Government* (London: Prime Minister's Strategy Unit, 2002).

6   All figures are excluding dependants.

7   Mark 12.28–34.

8   See Oliver O'Donovan, *Resurrection and Moral Order*, 2nd ed. (Leicester: Apollos, 1994).

9   For an extended and valuable study of the moral lessons to be learnt from the history and experience of the people of God, see Christopher Wright, *Old Testament Ethics for the People of God* (Leicester: IVP, 2004).

10 Michael Schluter, *Relationism: Pursuing a Biblical Vision for Society* (Cambridge Papers, Vol. 6, No. 4, December 1997).

2 Asylum

1   *Sun*, 18 August 2003.

2   *Independent*, 23 May 2003.

3   The most widely accepted definition of a refugee comes from the 1951 United Nations Convention relating to the Status of Refugees, extended in its application by the 1967 Protocol relating to the Status of Refugees, which defines a refugee as a person who 'owing to a well-founded fear of being persecuted for reasons of race, religion, nationality, membership of a particular social group or political opinion, is outside the country of his nationality and unable or, owing to such fear, is unwilling to avail himself of the protection of that country; or who, not having a nationality and being outside the country of his former habitual residence [. . .] is unable or, owing to such fear, is unwilling to return to it.'

4   <www.mori.com/polls/2002/refugee.shtml>. The correct answer to this question is itself very difficult to calculate. The global refugee population is a 'stock' figure, i.e. it gives the current stock of

refugees. Conversely, national refugee populations are often not measured and national asylum ones are 'flow' figures, i.e. they measure the year-on-year flow of asylum applications rather than the stock of refugees. Whatever the correct figure is, it is certainly less than 23 per cent.

5   <www.mori.com/digest/2000/pd001027.shtml>.

6   <www.mori.com/polls/2003/migration.shtml>.

7   See Home Office Research and Statistics: <www.homeoffice. gov.uk/rds>.

8   For this and other UNHCR statistics see www.unhcr.ch/cgi-bin/texis/vtx/statistics>.

9   S. Castles *et al.*, *States of Conflict: Causes and Patterns of Forced Migration to the EU and Policy Responses* (London: Institute for Public Policy Research, 2003).

10 A. Bradstock and A. Trotman (eds), *Asylum Voices* (London: Church House Publishing, 2003).

11 Exodus 12.38. It is no coincidence that the question of whether foreigners, slaves, temporary residents, hired workers, and aliens 'living among you' should be permitted to partake of Passover was settled, at least in narrative terms, immediately after the mention of the 'other people' in this verse.

12 Genesis 23.3–4.

13 Exodus 23.9; Leviticus 19.34; Deuteronomy 26.5; 1 Chronicles 29.15.

14 Leviticus 19.33–34.

15 Exodus 20.9–11; 22.21; 23.9.

16 Leviticus 19.9–10; 23.22; Deuteronomy 24.14–15, 19–22, 28–29; 26.12–13; Numbers 35.15; Ezekiel 47.21–23.

17 See, for example, Ezekiel 22.6–7, 29; Jeremiah 7.4–7; 22.3–5; Zechariah 7.10; Malachi 3.5.

18 Numbers 15.29–30; Leviticus 24.10–22; 18.26.

19 *Nokrim* were, for example, ineligible for the remission of debts, for kingship, for Passover, and for interest-free trading.

20 Matthew 25.34–40.

21 Luke 17.11–19.

22 Luke 9.51–56.

23 Acts 1.8.

24 Acts 8.4–25; 15.3–4.

25 1 Peter 1.1; 1.17; 2.11.

26 The aborted and much criticized asylum voucher scheme, which effectively alienated asylum seekers and transferred money from their pockets to shop tills through the widespread refusal to give change for transactions, is a good example of an unpalatable measure which, in spite of positive objectives, failed on pretty much every count.

27 One example of this: in May 2003, under a front-page banner headline 'Asylum: the facts', the *Independent* included the vignette, 'In 1999–2000 immigrants contributed £31.2bn in taxes and consumed £28.8bn in benefits – a net contribution of about £2.5bn to the economy' – a fact which has nothing whatsoever to do with asylum.

3 Race and Nationhood

1 Yasmin Alibhai-Brown, *True Colours: Public Attitudes to Multiculturalism and the Role of Government* (London: Institute for Public Policy Research, 1999).

2 At a press conference to launch its report, *Raising the Attainment of Minority Ethnic Pupils*, inspectors from the Office for Standards in Education claimed that many of Britain's schools were 'institutionally racist'. A separate report revealed that 'Britain's older universities [are] institutionally racist,' according to Tracy McVeigh ('"Racial bias" at UK's elite universities', *Guardian*, 23 June 2002). In an interview in June 2002, the Director of Public Prosecutions countered suggestions that the Crime Prosecution Service was racist by claiming 'that British society is institutionally racist . . . the whole of society has a problem'.

3 C. Rothon and A. Heath, 'Trends in racial prejudice', in *British Social Attitudes: The 20th Report*.

4 <www.cre.gov.uk/pdfs/moripoll.pdf>.

5 <www.mori.com/polls/trends/issues.shtml>.

6 Office for National Statistics, *UK 2003: The Official Yearbook of the United Kingdom and Northern Ireland* (London: Stationery Office, 2003), p. 124. Within this, there were wide variations between minority ethnic groups, with 24.2 per cent of those of Bangladeshi origin, 14.6 per cent of those of Black African origin and 6.2 per cent of those of Indian origin being unemployed.

7 23.7 vs. 10.6 per cent. See <www.statistics.gov.uk/cci/nugget.asp?id=409>.

8   <www.mori.com/polls/2003/migration.shtml>.

9   See Chapter 4.

10 *Community Cohesion: A Report of the Independent Review Team Chaired by Ted Cantle*, paragraph 5.1.15.

11 'A corrosive national danger in our multicultural model', *Guardian*, 6 November 2001.

12 Jonathan Sacks, *The Dignity of Difference* (London: Continuum, 2002).

13 Romans 11.1; Acts 16.37; 22.25–28; Colossians 3.11.

14 J. Daniel Hays, *From Every People and Nation: A Biblical Theology of Race* (Downers Grove: IVP, 2003); Richard Bauckham, *The Climax of Prophecy* (Edinburgh: T. & T. Clark, 1993).

15 The exception to this might seem to be the opening chapters of 1 Chronicles and the books of Ezra and Nehemiah, but these deal with very specific, post-exilic circumstances. See Nick Spencer, *Asylum and Immigration: A Christian Perspective on a Polarised Debate* (Carlisle: Paternoster, 2004) and Hays, *From Every People.*

16 N. T. Wright, *The New Testament and the People of God* (London: SPCK, 1992).

17 Deuteronomy 4.6.

18 John 18.36.

19 1 Peter 2.9.

20 Philippians 3.20.

21 Hebrew 11.13–16.

22 Revelation 3.12; 21.2, 14; 22.14, 19.

23 David Koyzis, *Political Visions and Illusions* (Downers Grove: IVP, 2003).

24 <www.mori.com/polls/2002/cre.shtml>.

25 The reaction of Trevor Phillips of the Commission for Racial Equality to David Goodhart's essay, 'Discomfort of strangers,' published in *Prospect* magazine and the *Guardian* in February 2004.

26 Roy Clements, *Where Love and Justice Meet* (Leicester: IVP, 1988).

27 Yasmin Alibhai-Brown, *Who Do We Think We Are?* (London: Penguin, 2000).

28 Migrants on works permits and their spouses cannot receive many benefits during their two-year probationary period.

29 The central argument of David Goodhart's essay, 'Discomfort of strangers'.

4 International Order

1 Samuel Huntington, *The Clash of Civilizations: And the Remaking of World Order* (Simon & Schuster, 1998).

2 Robert Kagan, *Paradise and Power* (London: Atlantic Books, 2003).

3 Romano Prodi, 13 April 1999, quoted in Ruth Lea, *The Essential Guide to the European Union* (London: Centre for Policy Studies, 2004).

4 Peter Heslam, *Globalization: Unravelling the New Capitalism* (Cambridge: Grove Books, 2002).

5 Roman Herzog, 'World domestic policy to build a global political system'; <www.dse.de/zeitschr/de399–5.htm>.

6 Roman Herzog, September 1996, quoted in Lea, *The Essential Guide*.

7 Robert Cooper, *The Breaking of Nations: Order and Chaos in the Twenty-First Century* (London: Atlantic Books, 2003).

8 Philip Bobbitt, *The Shield of Achilles: War, Peace and the Course of History* (London: Allen Lane, 2002). For Rowan Williams' comments on Bobbitt's thesis see <www.archbishopofcanterbury.org/sermons_speeches/2002/021219.html>.

9 Christopher Wright, *Old Testament Ethics for the People of God* (Leicester: IVP, 2004).

10 B. G. B Logsdon, *Multipolarity and Covenant: Towards a Biblical Framework for Constitutional Safeguards* (Cambridge: Jubilee Centre, 1989).

11 Deuteronomy 24.5; 17.14–20.

12 Ezekiel 31; Jeremiah 50.17–18; Isaiah 13–27; for Cyrus see Isaiah 44.28; 45.1, 13.

13 Jeremy Ive, 'Relationships in the Christian tradition', *Jubilee Manifesto*.

14 Ive, 'Relationships'.

15 Pius XI, *Quadragesimo Anno: On Reconstruction of the Social Order* (1931, paragraph 79); <www.osjspm.org/cst/qa.htm>.

16 <www.eurotreaties.com/maastrichteu.pdf>. Subsidiarity was defined in Article 3b of the Treaty establishing the European Community, in the following way: 'In areas which do not fall within its exclusive competence, the Community shall take action, in accordance with the principle of subsidiarity, only if and in so far as the objectives of the proposed action cannot be sufficiently achieved by the Member States and can therefore, by reason of the scale or effects of the proposed action, be better achieved by the Community.'

17 Quoted in John Wolffe, *God and Greater Britain: Religion and National*

Life in Britain and Ireland, 1843–1945 (London: Routledge, 1994).

18 Roger Scruton, *The Need for Nations* (London: Civitas, 2004).

19 For example, Pat Robertson, *The New World Order* (Milton Keynes: Word, 1992).

20 George Monbiot, *The Age of Consent* (London: HarperCollins, 2003).

21 <www.christian-aid.org.uk/news/stories/030502s.htm>.

22 Richard Harries, *Is There a Gospel for the Rich?* (London: Mowbray, 1992).

23 Revelation 5.9; 7.9; 11.9; 13.7; 14.6.

5 Education

1 There are, it should be noted, some reservations about whether this is actually true. A recent UK Graduate Careers Survey reported that the proportion of final-year students planning to go straight into a career job was lower in 2004 than at any time over the previous decade. A study from the British Chambers of Commerce reported that Britain's real skills shortage was not for degree-qualified workers but for skilled technicians in construction, engineering and information technology. A book by academics Phillip Brown and Anthony Hesketh entitled *The Mismanagement of Talent* seriously questioned the government's assumptions about the kinds of jobs graduates will end up in.

2 One reason why a 2004 report to the Welsh Assembly advised abolishing tests for 11–14-year-olds.

3 See, for example, 'So are A-levels getting easier?' <http://news.bbc. co.uk/1/hi/education/1495184.stm>.

4 HM Treasury and Cabinet Office, *Devolving Decision Making: 1. Delivering Better Public Services: Refining Targets and Performance Management* (March 2004), Chart 2.7; <www.hm-treasury.gov.uk/ media//53886/devolving_decision1_409.pdf>.

5 Rebecca Smithers, 'Disruptive pupils leave teachers battling to find a way to teach', *Guardian,* 27 May 2004.

6 See, for example, John MacBeath and Maurice Galton, *Life in Secondary Teaching* (Cambridge University Faculty of Education, 2004; <www.educ.cam.ac.uk/download/aLiSTreport.pdf>); Andi Wright and Katie Keetley, *Violence and Indiscipline in Schools: Research Study Commissioned by NASUWT* (Leicester: Perpetuity Research & Consultancy International, 2003; <image.guardian.co.uk/sys-files/

Education/documents/2003/10/17/NASUWTreport.pdf>).

7   <www.youth-justice-board.gov.uk/Publications/Downloads/
    YouthSurvey2003.pdf>.

8   <http://news.bbc.co.uk/1/hi/education/3564531.stm>.

9   Deuteronomy 6.1–7.

10   Deuteronomy 11.18–21.

11   Exodus 19.3–8.

12   Sacks, *Dignity of Difference.*

13   Proverbs 1.20–21; 3.15; 7.4; 8.6–14.

14   Proverbs 3.16.

15   Proverbs 3.14.

16   Proverbs 3.17–18.

17   Proverbs 3.19–20.

18   E.g. Psalm 8; 19.1–2.

19   Ecclesiastes 3.1–8.

20   John 1.1–14.

21   Romans 1.20.

22   1 Kings 4.33.

23   Wisdom of Solomon 7.17–22.

24   Thus Francis Bacon (1561–1626): 'There are two books laid before
    us to study, to prevent our falling into error; first, the volume of the
    Scriptures, which reveal the will of God; then the volume of the
    Creatures, which express His power.'

25   Alister McGrath, *Nature* (London: T. & T. Clark, 2001).

26   Proverbs 4.6–11.

27   Ephesians 4.11.

28   2 Timothy 3.14–17; see also 1 Timothy 4.11–14.

29   Psalms 1.2; 119.97; Proverbs 4.6.

30   Colossians 1.10.

31   Matthew Arnold, '*Culture and Anarchy' and Other Writings,* ed. Stefan
    Collini (Cambridge: Cambridge University Press, 1993).

32   <www.legislation.hmso.gov.uk/acts/acts1988/Ukpga_19880040_
    en_2.htm#mdiv1>; Nestlé Family Monitor, *Young People's Attitudes
    towards Politics* (MORI, 2003: <www.mori.com/polls/2003/pdf/
    nfm16_trust.pdf>); Nestlé Family Monitor: *Mapping Britain's Moral
    Values* (MORI, 2000: <www.mori.com/polls/2000/pdf/nfm08.
    pdf>).

6 Transport and Mobility

1 *Transport Trends 2003*, 2.3, <www.dft.gov.uk/stellent/groups/ dft_transstats/documents/downloadable/dft_transstats_026279.pdf>.

2 *Transport Trends 2001*, Tables 1.1 and 3.4 <www.dft.gov.uk/stellent/ groups/dft_control/documents/contentservertemplate/dft_index. hcst?n=7683&1=3>.

3 *Transport Trends 2003*, 1.1, <www.dft.gov.uk/stellent/groups/ dft_transstats/documents/downloadable/dft_transstats_026279.pdf>.

4 *Transport Trends 2003*, 6.1, <www.dft.gov.uk/stellent/groups/dft_ transstats/documents/downloadable/dft_transstats_026279.pdf>.

5 Felicity Lawrence, *Not on the Label* (London: Penguin, 2004).

6 <www.statistics.gov.uk/StatBase/tsdataset.asp?vlnk=704&Pos= 1&ColRank=1&Rank=272>.

7 The following paragraphs draw heavily on John Adams, *The Social Implications of Hypermobility* <www.geog.ucl.ac.uk/~jadams/publish. htm>.

8 Mayer Hillman (ed.), *Children, Transport and the Quality of Life* (London: Policy Studies Institute, 1993), quoted in *The Social Implications of Hypermobility*, <www.geog.ucl.ac.uk/v.jabams/publish.htm>.

9 DETR Transport Statistics (<www.transtat.dft.gov.uk/index.htm>).

10 Tom Wolfe, *A Man in Full* (London: Jonathan Cape, 1998).

11 We do hear of Solomon's successful fleet of trading ships in 1 Kings 10.22, but also of Jehoshaphat's that never got out of port (1 Kings 22.48). For enforced travel see the exodus (Exodus 12), the exile (2 Chronicles 36) and the early persecution of the church (Acts 8.2).

12 Genesis 4.1–14.

13 Genesis 12.1–3.

14 John 1.46; Matthew 8.20.

15 Numbers 26; 34; Joshua 13—19; Leviticus 25; Deuteronomy 27.17; Hosea 5.10.

16 Micah 2.2.

17 Amos 8.4.

18 Isaiah 5.2.

19 Leviticus 25.23.

20 See, for example, 1 Chronicles 29.15; Psalm 90.10.

21 Matthew 8.20.

22 Luke 10.25–37.

23 See the Department of Transport's Home Zone Challenge, <www.dft.

gov.uk/stellent/groups/dft_susttravel/documents/page/dft_susttravel_504007.hcsp>.

7 Health and Healthcare

1 Quoted in Beth Egan, 'Comparing Health Systems', *Prospect*, April 2002.

2 Sonia Exley and Lindsey Jarvis, *Trends in Attitudes to Health Care 1983 to 2000* (National Centre for Social Research, 2002) (Table 2.1).

3 P. Taylor-Gooby and C. Hastie, 'Support for state spending: has New Labour got it right?', in *British Social Attitudes: The 19th Report*.

4 *Budget 2002: The Strength to make Long-Term Decisions*, 17 April 2002.

5 J. Appleby and A. Rosete, 'The NHS: keeping up with public expectations?', in *British Social Attitudes: The 20th Report*.

6 Appleby and Rosete, 'The NHS: keeping up with public expectations?'

7 *Reforming our Public Services* (The Prime Minister's Office of Public Service Reform: <www.pm.gov.uk/files/pdf/Principles.pdf>).

8 *Reforming our Public Services.*

9 See Leviticus 4.11–12; 7.15–19; 11.7; 11.13–19; 11.39–40; 13.1–46; 17.15–16; 19.6–7.

10 A. Darling, 'The Levitical Code: Hygiene or Holiness', in *Medicine and the Bible*, ed. B. Palmer (Exeter: Paternoster Press, 1986).

11 Roy Porter, *The Greatest Benefit to Mankind* (London: Fontana, 1997).

12 Ian McColl, 'National Priorities for Health', in *Our National Life*, ed. Allister Vale (London: Monarch Books, 1998).

13 Andrew Fergusson (ed.), *Health: The Strength to be Human* (Leicester: IVP, 1993).

14 Fergusson, *Health*, pp. 25–26; David J. Atkinson and David H. Field (eds.), *New Dictionary of Christian Ethics and Pastoral Theology* (Leicester: IVP, 1995), pp. 435–437.

15 For an example of an interesting movement in medical history that reflects this viewpoint, see on the 'patient-as-a-person' movement in Porter, *Greatest Benefit*, pp. 682–686.

16 See Deuteronomy 4.6.

17 See Deuteronomy 15.7; 15.11; 17.15; Romans 12.1; 15.14; 15.30; 16.17.

18 Galatians 6.2.

19   Sacks, *Dignity of Difference*.

20   Sacks, *Dignity of Difference*.

21   See Updated Drugs Strategy 2002, <http://image.guardian. co.uk/sys-files/Guardian/documents/2002/12/03/Updated_Drug_ Strategy_2002.pdf>.

22   At least five times a week, according to the government's chief medical officer; see <image.guardian.co.uk/sys-files/Society/documents/ 2004/04/29/At_least5aweek.pdf>.

23   At least five portions of fresh fruit and vegetables every day, according to a scheme re-launched in 2003.

24   See Prime Minister's Strategy Unit, *Alcohol Harm Reduction Strategy For England*, <http://image.guardian.co.uk/sys-files/Society/ documents/2004/03/15/alcoholstrategy.pdf>.

25   See Silver Ring Thing: <www.silverringthing.com/>.

26   See, for example, Anna Coote, *Prevention Rather than Cure* (London: King's Fund, 2004; <image.guardian.co.uk/sys-files/Society/ documents/2004/03/18/Prevention.pdf>); Derek Wanless, *Securing Good Health for the Whole Population* (London: Stationery Office, 2004; <www.hm-treasury.gov.uk/consultations_and_legislation/ wanless/consult_wanless04_final.cfm>).

27   Wanless, *Securing Good Health*.

28   See Geoffrey Meads and John Ashcroft, *The Case for Collaboration by Health and Social Care Professionals* (Oxford: Blackwell, 2004).

29   See Michael Schluter and David Lee, *The R Option* (Cambridge: Relationships Foundation, 2003); Michael Schluter and David Lee, *The R Factor* (London: Hodder & Stoughton, 2003).

30   Quoted in Fergusson, *Health*.

8 Criminal Justice

1   New Labour 1997 Election Manifesto: *Because Britain Deserves Better*; 2001 Election Manifesto: *Ambitions for Britain*.

2   Crime statistics are notoriously controversial and must be treated with caution. UK Crime levels are measured in two ways. The British Crime Survey (BCS) interviews 40,000 adults per year, asks them about the crimes they experienced in the last 12 months and grosses up the results to estimate the total number of crimes committed in the UK in that period. The Recorded Crime Statistics records all 'notifiable' offences recorded by the police. The two differ in that the former includes crimes that are not reported to the

police, and thus records a far higher level of crime. For more details see <www.homeoffice.gov.uk/rds/patterns1.html>.

3 J. Simmons and T. Dodd (eds), *Crime in England and Wales 2002/3* (Home Office Statistical Bulletin, July 2003: <www.homeoffice. gov.uk/rds/crimeew0203.html>, Tables 3.01 (BCS) and 3.04 (Recorded Crime). It should be noted that BCS trends differ from the Recorded Crime Statistics, which show an increase from 4.6 million recorded crimes in 1997 to 5.9 million in 2002/3.

4 Simmons, *Crime*, Tables 3.01 and 3.02.

5 Simmons, *Crime*, Figure 8.1.

6 Simmons, *Crime*, Figure 8.2.

7 I.e. the total number of crimes reported to the police, not the (calculated) total number of crimes committed.

8 Simmons, *Crime*, Section 7.1. Detected crimes are, broadly speaking, those that have been 'cleared up' by the police; cf. Simmons, *Crime*, p. 110, for details.

9 Simmons, *Crime,* Table 3.05; J. Hicks and G. Allen, *A Century of Change: Trends in UK Statistics since 1900* (House of Commons Research Paper 99/111), Sections V and VI. It should be noted that the proportion of crimes reported has almost certainly increased over this period and so the rise in crime levels is unlikely to be as steep as it first appears.

10 MORI surveys since the late 1970s have consistently shown that a majority of the British population favours the death penalty in some circumstances, such as the murder of children, although this majority can disappear according to how the question is asked; see <www.mori.com/mrr/2002/c020823.shtml>.

11 Sunder Katwala, 'So where are the big ideas?', *Observer*, 27 April 2003.

12 Jeremiah 9.24.

13 Bruce Malchow, *Social Justice in the Hebrew Bible* (Minnesota: The Liturgical Press, 1996), quoted in Michael Schluter, 'Three Relationional Dimensions of Justice', in *Christian Perspectives on Law and Relationism*, ed. P. Beaumont and K. Wotherspoon (Carlisle: Paternoster Press, 2000).

14 Schluter, *Christian Perspectives.*

15 Exodus 5.1; 40.34.

16 E.g. Hebrews 2.11–13; Ephesians 2.16; Colossians 1.20; Romans 8.21; 2 Corinthians 5.17, etc.

17 Exodus 21.12–36.
18 Jonathan Burnside, 'Criminal Justice', in *Jubilee Manifesto.*
19 Deuteronomy 13.11; 21.21.
20 Deuteronomy 16.20.
21 Deuteronomy 27.19.
22 Deuteronomy 1.17.
23 Exodus 18.21.
24 Deuteronomy 17.6.
25 Deuteronomy 16.18.
26 Exodus 24.3; Deuteronomy 1.1.
27 Deuteronomy 27.1–3; 6.4–12; 31.9–11.
28 Leviticus 5.1.
29 Numbers 35.30; Deuteronomy 17.6; 19.15; 17.7.
30 Deuteronomy 25.1–3.
31 Christopher Townsend, *An Eye for an Eye? The Morality of Punishment* (Cambridge Papers, Vol. 6, No. 1, March 1997); see Exodus 22.1, 4, 7.
32 Exodus 21.18–19.
33 1 Peter 2.14.
34 Galatians 6.2; 1 Corinthians 8.9.
35 Matthew 18.15–17.
36 1 Corinthians 5.13; cf. Deuteronomy 17.7; 19.19; 21.21; 22.21, 24; 24.7.
37 2 Corinthians 2.5–8.
38 1 Timothy 5.19–20.
39 1 Thessalonians 3.14–15.
40 Numbers 35.6, 11, 13.
41 D. Garland, *The Culture of Control: Crime and Social Order in Contemporary Society* (Oxford: Oxford University Press, 2001).
42 <www.socialexclusionunit.gov.uk>.
43 Oliver Letwin, *Beyond the Causes of Crime* (London: Centre for Policy Studies, 2002).
44 See David Halpern and Clive Bates, *Personal Responsibility and Changing Behaviour: The State of Knowledge and its Implications for Public Policy* (London: Prime Minister's Strategy Unit, 2004).
45 Burnside, 'Criminal Justice'.
46 The following figures are drawn from the Prison Reform Trust March 2004 Briefing Paper.
47 S. Maruna *et al.*, 'The prisoner's beatitude', *Relational Justice Bulletin* 14 (2002).

48 Philip Johnston, 'Christian wings in jails win reprieve', *Daily Telegraph*, 5 March 2002; see Jonathan Burnside *et al.*, *Religion & Rehabilitation: Faith-Based Therapeutic Communities in Prison* (Cullompton: Willan Publishing, forthcoming)

49 D. Faulkner, 'Crime, citizenship and community', *Relational Justice Bulletin* 18 (2003).

9 The Economy

1 The posters had slogans such as 'The Repossessed: No home is safe from spiralling Tory interest rates'.

2 CPI – Consumer Prices Index – inflation is the new inflationary measure, as announced by the Chancellor in 2003. It differs from the old RPI – Retail Prices Index – measure in a number of ways, such as excluding certain housing costs, covering all private households and utilizing some specific differences in price measurement. For further details, see <www.statistics.gov.uk/cci/nugget.asp?id=181>.

3 M. Brewer *et al.*, *Poverty and Inequality in Britain: 2004* (London: Institute for Fiscal Studies, 2004).

4 That is after housing costs; see Brewer *et al.*, *Poverty and Inequality*, Box 2.1, Tables 3.1, 3.2.

5 See Michael Moynagh and Richard Worsley, *The Opportunity of a Lifetime: Reshaping Retirement* (Tomorrow Project/CIPD, 2004).

6 See, for example, <www.andrewoswald.com>; Reeves, *The Politics of Happiness*; Hamilton, *Growth Fetish*; Layard, *Happiness*.

7 P. Dickman (ed.), *Economic Trends Annual Supplement, No. 29* (Office for National Statistics, 2003; <www.statistics.gov.uk/downloads/theme_economy/ETAS02.pdf>).

8 Layard, *Happiness.*

9 *Life Satisfaction: The State of Knowledge and Implications for Government* (London: Prime Minister's Strategy Unit, 2002).

10 For a more detailed analysis of this see Nick Spencer, *The Measure of All Things? A Biblical Perspective on Money and Value in Britain Today* (Cambridge: Jubilee Centre, 2003).

11 Ecclesiastes 5.19; 8.15; 11.8.

12 Matthew 6.34; Luke 12.16–21; James 4.13–17.

13 1 Chronicles 29.14–16.

14 Matthew 19.16–30; 6.19–21; cf. James 5.2.

15 1 Timothy 6.7–9.

16 Matthew 22.37–38.

17   Proverbs 31.10–31.
18   Luke 16.9.
19   Ephesians 4.28.
20   The following paragraphs draw heavily on Paul Mills' chapter on the economy in *Jubilee Manifesto*.
21   Spencer, *Asylum and Immigration*.
22   The following statistics are taken from Credit Action: <www.creditaction.org.uk>.
23   *Fair, Clear and Competitive – The Consumer Credit Market in the 21st Century* <www.dti.gov.uk/ccp/topics1/consumer_finance.htm>.
24   *Shows Promise. But Must Try Harder* (Sustainable Development Commission, 2004: <www.sd-commission.gov.uk/pubs/assessment/pdf/assessment.pdf>).
25   Jil Matheson and Carol Summerfield (eds), *Social Trends* 31 (Office for National Statistics, 2001), Table 4.8; see Madeleine Bunting, *Willing Slaves* (London: HarperCollins, 2004).
26   Economic and Social Research Council, Future of Work programme: <www.leeds.ac.uk/esrcfutureofwork/>.
27   Kate Bishop, 'Working time patterns in the UK, France, Denmark and Sweden', *Labour Market Trends*, Vol. 112, No.3: <www.statistics.gov.uk/articles/labour_market_trends/Working_time_patterns.pdf>.
28   According to the *World Competitiveness Yearbook 2004* (Lausanne: International Institute for Management Development, 2004), Denmark comes 7th, Sweden 11th, UK 22nd, and France 30th in terms of competitiveness; see <www.imd.ch/wcy>. According to the *United Nations Development Report 2003* (Oxford: Oxford University Press, 2003), Denmark comes 4th, France 16th, UK 20th and Sweden 21st in terms of GDP per capita <www.undp.org>. It should be noted, however, that, at least according to one recent survey, the majority of small-company bosses in France think the compulsory 35-hour week is having an adverse effect on the country's economy (see <http://news.bbc.co.uk/1/hi/business/3911009.stm>).
29   *Private Action, Public Benefit: A Review of Charities and the Wider Not-For-Profit Sector* (London: Prime Minister's Strategy Unit, 2002: <www.number-10.gov.uk/su/voluntary/report/index.htm>); see also, 'Give and Take' (*Analysis*, Radio 4, first broadcast 15 July 2004).
30   <http://hdr.undp.org>.
31   See Hamilton, *Growth Fetish*.

32 *Chasing Progress: Beyond Measuring Economic Growth* (London: New Economics Foundation, 2004).

33 See David Boyle, *Funny Money: In Search of Alternative Cash* (London: HarperCollins, 1999); Time banks: <www.timebanks.co.uk>; and especially the work of the New Economics Foundation: <www.neweconomics.org>.

34 See <www.care-for-the-family.org.uk>.

Conclusion: Voting Wisely

1 Dan Corry and Gerry Stoker, *New Localism: Refashioning the Centre–Local Relationship* (London: New Local Government Network, 2002).